OCCASIONAL  AFFAIRS

T. THE LAW IN POLITICAL INTEGRATION

The Evolution and Integrative Implications of Regional

Legal Processes in the European Community

By *Stuart A. Scheingold*

with

FOREWORD

By

Ernst B. Haas

Published by the

Center for International Affairs

Harvard University

ABOUT THE AUTHOR

Stuart A. Scheingold is Associate Professor of Political Science at the University of Washington. He received his Ph.D. from the University of California at Berkeley and has taught at the University of Wisconsin and at the Davis Campus of the University of California. Professor Scheingold has been a Social Science Research Council Fellow and was Research Associate at the Center for International Affairs. His published writings include *The Rule of Law in European Integration: The Path of the Schuman Plan* (1965) and *Europe's Would-Be Polity: Patterns of Change in the European Community* (with Leon N. Lindberg, 1970). He is also a contributor to and co-editor (with Professor Lindberg) of *Regional Integration: Theory and Research* (1971).

We are usually told that government by laws is preferable to government by men. Law is abstract and impersonal; when it is capricious it dispenses its caprice without personal animus. Politics — government by men — is down-to-earth and highly personal; political decisions imply the ready use of arbitrary power. In short, law is good and government (politics) much less so.

This preference for law has found its way into studies of regional integration. We see it also in schemes for banishing power politics from international relations. Law is thought to permit the peaceful definition of points in dispute and the orderly settlement of the issue by means of third-party intercession, constitutionally anchored in a dignified tribunal. Politics, on the other hand, is concerned merely with the assertion of self-interest by the parties to a dispute; at best it succeeds in settling their dispute peacefully after bluff, threat, and saber-rattling, but without recourse to principles of justice and order that reach beyond their self-interest. Advocates of "world peace through world law" thus see in a rejuvenated World Court and in the repeal of the Connally Reservation the key to the kingdom of peace. Similarly, many friends of regional unification in Europe see in the role of the European Court and the system of law which accompanies the Treaties of Paris and Rome the beginning of a new type of regional polity, a more ethical and humane system.

Stuart A. Scheingold makes very clear in this volume why both are wrong. He shows beyond any doubt that, far from having taken the place of regional politics, European regional law has in fact permitted politics to operate at the regional level in the form of greater discretion for the regional executive. He also shows why there has been no recourse to litigation in the most severe disputes among the members of the European Community. For those who are tempted to use the constitutional history of the United States as their model for studying the progress of European integration, Professor Scheingold offers some sobering thoughts. The work of the European Court of Justice cannot be meaningfully studied against the backdrop of John Marshall's Supreme Court, or even Earl Warren's. The building of an authoritative and legitimate federation — in the absence of consistent political leadership — can certainly profit from, and, some would say, depends on, a type of judicial activism which would turn the judiciary into the federalizing catalyst. Professor Scheingold shows us why the American model does not apply to the European experience. More important, he shows that judicial activism and self-conscious federalizing would have hampered integration rather than helped it.

In demonstrating the irrelevance of the approaches suggesting legal and judicial supremacy over politics and politicians, Professor Scheingold offers a pioneering analysis which argues a far more subtle role for law, lawyers, and judges in the process of regional integration. Judges forswearing judicial activism can nonetheless link regional with national law even if the question of supremacy is not finally settled. More important, they can so link these levels as to encourage the politicians to continue to bargain with one another until a settlement is reached. However, once the new *règlement* is in effect the consensual-bargaining flavor of regional decisionmaking yields to coercion and, in that sense, even the consensual process of regional politics resembles federal practice. Hence it is of the greatest interest to learn how attorneys, in their role of habituating their clients to such regimes, have reacted to the evolution of a continental economic law. Professor Scheingold presents a unique body of information on the attitudinal adaptations of European attorneys, all the more impressive because the Dutch, French, German, Italian, and Belgian bar had none of the crutches which the common law and the Privy Council provided to earlier generations of American, Australian, and Canadian lawyers who sought to work and live with a federation.

This study is an important addition to a growing body of data on the informal processes of integration which seem to be going on in Europe even in the absence of federal law and practice. If federation is not politically desired and if the federal judicial model is inappropriate in explaining what is actually happening, the changing habits of interest groups, the growing indifference of youth to national symbols, the pairing of cities and universities take their place alongside the habits of attorneys and their clients in suggesting what is really occurring. All these trends suggest tolerance for integration, not enthusiasm. Hence they reenforce the questions Professor Scheingold persistently asks: how sturdy is all this, is it reversible, can it persist on the basis of bargaining and compromise and without a central authority? He cannot yet answer these questions. But if we exclude the authority that goes with federal law and federally-sanctioned coercion, we are as scholars forced to address ourselves to them. This work is an important step in the right direction.

ERNST B. HAAS
*University of California
at Berkeley*

ACKNOWLEDGEMENTS

This project would not have been possible without the very generous support of the Center for International Affairs at Harvard University. I am also indebted to its staff, faculty, and research associates for counsel and encouragement — in particular to Stanley Hoffmann, Joseph S. Nye, Benjamin Brown, Robert Erwin, and Marina S. Finkelstein. I am especially grateful to Eric Stein, who has commented in detail on earlier drafts, and to Kozo Yamamura and John Brode, who were immensely helpful with data processing and analysis. Others who have been generous with their time and considerate with their criticism at various stages of the project are Ernst B. Haas, Richard M. Buxbaum, Leon N. Lindberg, Sergio Neri, and Claus-Dieter Ehlermann. Raymond Baeyens has been kind and helpful in numerous ways over a long period of time. An earlier draft of this paper was delivered at the Sixty-sixth Annual Meeting of the American Political Science Association, September 8–12, 1970. Portions of the material were presented to the Conference on Law as an Obstacle to Social Change at Wayne State University, May 24–25, 1968. The National Securities Studies Group of the University of Wisconsin, Madison, also provided financial assistance for this work.

TABLE OF CONTENTS

LIST OF TABLES

FIGURES

1. Introduction

The purpose of this paper is to assess the status and role of legal processes in the political integration of the European Community.[1] The study is guided in part by a spirit of summary and synthesis, but only a partial balance sheet will be offered. The focus is narrowed by my political perspective and by my empirical concerns. More specifically, there are two propositions I wish to argue and defend:

1. The political analysis of Community legal processes should extend beyond a consideration of the judgments of its "supreme courts." More specifically, other participants in the legal processes should be investigated and, in addition, an attempt should be made to determine how judicial decisions feed generally into the Community political process.

2. The federal teleology which has crept into the work of so many of us concerned with the political implications of legal processes should be abandoned. We should cease asking whether or not judicial decisions are promoting the primacy of regional institutions within a framework of constitutional norms. Instead we ought to learn more about the way in which the law relates to the non-federal and more consensual patterns that seem to be taking shape within the Community.

In this sort of enterprise, the traditional tool of legal inquiry — rigorous textual analysis — is only tangentially relevant.[2] Consequently, I shall not enter into the debates among legal scholars relating to doctrinal developments or into disputes among stu-

[1]

dents of the civil and common law having to do with such problems as judicial activism.[3] In sum, this is neither a brief legal history of the European Community nor does it attempt a comprehensive review of the voluminous literature on the legal aspects of European integration.[4] The boundaries of the paper are, instead, defined by the two propositions set forth above. Let us consider each of them in detail before going on to look at the data.

The Court of Justice

The first proposition is a reaction to the narrow scope of most research on the political implications of the law in the European Community. The primary institutional focus has been the Community's Court of Justice. This tribunal — a kind of Community "supreme court" — has been handing down binding judgments since 1954. All six member-governments as well as some of the largest corporations in Europe have been parties to litigation before this tribunal, which sits in Luxembourg.[5] Many of the major conflicts of the Community have come to the Court. The record of compliance with its judicial decisions has been exceedingly good by any standards.[6] It is, therefore, hardly surprising that the Court of Justice has been viewed as *the* important point of convergence between law and politics within the European Community and, accordingly, as the institution upon which to concentrate the most attention.

While understandable and quite sensible, this approach also raises some important problems. The judgments of the Court of Justice are the most visible and accessible aspect of the legal process. They may even comprise the "constitutional law" of the European Community. But are they the operative norms of the Community system? The question extends beyond the matter of compliance with individual decisions. The more important issue is whether countless numbers of analogous transactions tend to be controlled by the principles used by the Court to deal with "leading" cases which come before the judges.

The problem, then, is to reach beyond the words of the judgments to behavior patterns developing in the Community. More specifically, the problem is to determine the role of law in the making of Community policy and the impact of law upon the emerging structures of authority in the Community.[7] Short of

[2]

detailed analysis of a variety of problem areas, any such effort must rest heavily, but not unreasonably, upon inference from aggregate figures on litigation before both the Court of Justice and the national courts. In addition, it is revealing to investigate the attitudes and behavior of private attorneys who are key participants in the Community legal process.[8] The shift in emphasis from the Court of Justice to the "grass roots" was, in my judgment, particularly useful for understanding the interaction of Community and national legal processes. In particular, the responses of the attorneys provided clues to changes in the patterns of authority that may be taking place within the European Community.

Federal Models

As for the second proposition, federal standards have often been applied to the work of the Court of Justice. The federal perspective has been exhaustively developed and applied most recently by Andrew W. Green, who assesses the contribution of the Court of Justice to political integration as follows:

> The elements of political integration which the Court of Justice increased in the European Communities are:
>
> (a) the jurisdiction of the Court of Justice;
> (b) the authority of the High Authority of the European Coal and Steel Community and the authority of the Commission of the European Economic Community;
> (c) the application of Community law directly to individuals;
> (d) the creation of an independent system of law;
> (e) the resolution of disputes and conflicts between member-states.[9]

In my judgment, however, neither the logic of the situation nor the available evidence suggests that the federal perspective is the most useful way of coming to grips with the integrative role of law. I am, in fact, increasingly skeptical about the utility of looking at the Court of Justice as a "federalizer."

The Community legal process, it is true, does have a strongly federal cast and, as we shall see, the Court of Justice has vigorously asserted federal prerogatives. Nevertheless, the system as a whole can not presently be characterized as a federal regime, since it does not conform to the traditional federal model either in terms of its decisionmaking structure or in terms of its functional responsibilities. Nor can it any longer be tacitly assumed that the

[3]

European Community is, or should be, moving toward a federal solution. The simple fact is that Community institutions are rather curiously ambivalent. The legal process seems to incorporate the member-states into a federal system. But the political process is basically consensual and pays more than lip service to the autonomy and integrity of national units in decisionmaking.

One could easily make too much of this ambivalence, regarding it either as a disabling contradiction or as an opportunity for judicial initiatives in behalf of federal ordering. I detect instead an interesting adjustment in which federal prerogatives have been asserted and established by the Court of Justice; but they have been employed very sparingly and then not so much in the service of the coercive patterns which typify the federal model as in support of the consensual politics of neofunctional processes. That is to say, I see evidence that the legal system is feeding into the symbiotic relationships emerging between community institutions and existing national structures — mobilizing national elites, enlisting national institutions in behalf of Community goals, and generally blurring the lines which divide one set of structures from the other.

Format

This paper is divided into two substantive sections. The purpose of the first is to reevaluate the federal perspective. More precisely, this section reviews the manner in which the Court of Justice has asserted federal prerogatives and then goes on to assess the actual role of the Court in the policymaking processes. The second section offers the alternative or consensual approach and presents data which suggest that the legal system may be enlisting national judges, mobilizing an important elite group, and engendering the participation in Community processes of a large and varied group of individuals and business interests.

Finally, before beginning the analysis let me add a few caveats. This paper presents neither a theory nor a paradigm. In part, it is simply a reinterpretation of what we already know. But it also presents new data within a frame of reference which departs from the usual approach to the role of law in the process of political integration. As such, it suggests a number of ways in which, in addition to its federalizing capacities, the law may be contributing to integration. Perhaps the major purpose of this

[4]

kind of exercise is to bare the need for more elaborate conceptualization or to indicate the kinds of data which are still to be collected. Perhaps it will simply suggest a new track for future research efforts. At the very least it will, I hope, point up the possibility and desirability of transcending the federal perspective.

2. THE FEDERAL PERSPECTIVE

The essential objective of the federalizing process is not necessarily different from other approaches to integration. The goal is simply a system which will promote the enduring and active commitment of the member-states to the common goals specified in the Community treaties. The distinctive feature of the federal perspective is its preoccupation with hierarchical patterns of authority, formal institutions, and legal processes. The legal instruments of federalization in the European Community are: (1) the primacy of Community law; (2) the direct applicability of Community rules within the member-states; and (3) the incorporation of private parties as subjects of Community law. The basic thrust of these innovations is to alter the status of the states in international law. In the first place, individuals, as such, are granted rights under the Community treaties and may assert these rights even against the member-states. In addition, the treaties take precedence over national law and, as we shall see, the Court of Justice is entrusted with the job of determining the rights and obligations of the states under these treaties. In sum, the federal forms set forth in the Community treaties imply the establishment of the "rule of law." They are all to be mutually and reciprocally constrained by the same set of rules and accountable to one another before a common judicial tribunal.

The doctrinal development of these federal prerogatives in the European Community has been considered at great length

[6]

in a number of studies by both lawyers and political scientists.[10] In this paper, I wish to discuss such doctrinal developments rather briefly, merely to indicate how vigorously the Court of Justice has asserted federal prerogatives. The more basic purpose of this discussion is to pave the way for a consideration of the actual imposition of constitutional obligations upon the participants in the integrative process. That is to say, I want to distinguish between the words of the Court and its deeds — between the assertion of federal prerogatives and the growth of federal patterns. To assert prerogatives in leading cases is to do no more than to open the channels. If we are really to understand the emerging system, we must learn how these channels are being utilized.

The Assertion of Federal Prerogatives

Let us consider, first, the novel position of private parties as subjects of the treaties of the European Community. As such, the private parties have both rights and obligations stemming directly from the treaties and from measures adopted by Community institutions and member-governments in pursuance of the treaties. What is perhaps most important from the federal perspective is the right of private parties to challenge the policy decisions of member-governments and Community institutions. The precise scope of this right varies from treaty to treaty and even among different provisions of the same treaty, but some general points can be made.

In the earliest cases arising under the Coal and Steel Community, the Court of Justice employed a flexible interpretation of that treaty to provide a rather open forum for private parties — in this case coal and steel enterprises and trade associations.[11] Without going into detail, suffice it to say that these firms were permitted to subject to judicial scrutiny and treaty standards most acts which impinged on their interests — whether taken by the Community executive (the High Authority), the member-governments, or another enterprise.[12]

Since these initial Coal and Steel Community judgments, the adjudicatory rights of private parties have been altered significantly — expanded in some ways and contracted in others. The rights of direct appeal to the Court of Justice have been clearly curtailed. The drafters of the Common Market treaty

[7]

implicitly rebuked the Court for its movement in the direction of the "interest" theory and specified that private parties shall have the right to bring suit in the Court of Justice only against acts applying to them or which concern them *directly* and *individually*.[13] The Court has rigorously adhered to this limitation in Common Market litigation and has even shown some signs of restricting access under the Coal and Steel Community Treaty.[14]

In contrast, the judges have been very responsive to individuals in litigation arising under a provision of the E.E.C. Treaty authorizing interlocutory judgments. This procedure enables, and in some cases requires, national judges to interrupt national litigation in order to get interpretations of Community rules from the Court of Justice.[15] The Court of Justice has been extraordinarily receptive to such requests and as a result individuals can, in effect, get a hearing before the Court of Justice. The best indicator of the receptivity of Community judges to these requests is the flexible approach they have taken to the procedural rules prescribing just how such questions are to be sent forward by the national judges. The Court of Justice has been willing to accept virtually all requests without regard to what seem to be irregularities of form. Similarly, the Court has not attempted to determine whether the national court had jurisdiction to consider the case or whether the question sent forward was relevant to the decision in the national court. In one early case, for example, the Court's Advocate General noted that despite the fact that the trial judges had failed to specify the questions which the Court was to consider, the problem could be treated.[16] More recently the Court of Justice willingly interpreted a provision of the Community Treaty for an Italian court despite the fact that, from all appearances, the article in question was unrelated to the issue being litigated.[17] Thus, while the remedy of direct appeal to the Court of Justice has been narrowed if not altogether foreclosed, a surrogate has been provided which is generally effective and in many respects more convenient than a separate action before the Court of Justice.[18]

Initially, there seemed to be persuasive reasons for doubting the utility of these interlocutory proceedings for vindicating the rights of private parties. Only if Community law were directly applicable in the member-states, of course, could it enter into national litigation. Most legal experts, however, believed that the Common Market Treaty was only a framework treaty (*traité*

[8]

cadre), which set forth general principles and obligated the governments to seek joint policies for implementation. In other words, one might well have wondered whether the Treaty, as such, had any direct impact on individuals. The Court stilled this concern in one of the first cases brought to it by way of Article 177. The details of this landmark decision are less important than the principles affirmed by the judges:

> The Community constitutes a new legal order in international law, for whose benefit the States have limited their sovereign rights, albeit within limited fields, and the subjects of which comprise not only the member-States but also their nationals. Community law, therefore, apart from legislation by the member-States, not only imposes obligations on individuals but also confers on them legal rights.[19]

The Court did not declare that *all* provisions of the Treaty were immediately and directly applicable and in later cases guidelines have been offered to national judges. As summarized by Advocate General Gand, if they are to be considered immediately and directly applicable,

> the obligations imposed on the member-State should be precise and unqualified, should not require any legal action by E.E.C. institutions to be brought into effect, and finally, should not leave member-States any real discretionary powers as to its implementation.[20]

Clearly guidance of this sort can not close all the loopholes, but what is important for our purposes is that major portions of the Treaty are thus opened to direct application

The *primacy of the Treaty* has been spelled out in at least two different ways by the Court of Justice. In the first place, the Court has spoken out strongly against governments that have responded in the classic manner to trade emergencies — that is by taking the law into their own hands and cutting off trade, providing export subsidies, etc. The judges have been adamant in their assault on this unilateralism. Whatever may be the substantive lacunae of the Treaty, it is according to the judges procedurally complete, for it provides ways of dealing with all problems. Unilateralism may have a place in the Treaty but it is a very small sanctuary, narrowly circumscribed by the provisions of Article 36.[21] When unspecified forms of emergency arise, the states are obligated to play the game according to the rules as they are formulated in, for example, Articles 226 and 235.[22]

[9]

The Court has also asserted the supremacy of Community law in relation to national legislative acts. Such primacy was declared in a 1964 case originating in Italy and involving an attack on the nationalization of the Italian electric industry. Although the Court did not rule against nationalization, it did hold that Community law took precedence over subsequent conflicting national legislation:

> In fact, by creating a Community of unlimited duration, having its own institutions, its own personality and its own capacity in law, apart from having international standing and more particularly, real powers resulting from a limitation of competence or a transfer of powers from the States to the Community, the member-States, albeit within limited spheres, have restricted their sovereign rights and created a body of law applicable both to their nationals and to themselves. The reception, within the laws of each member-State, of provisions having a Community source, and more particularly of the terms and of the spirit of the Treaty, has as a corollary the impossibility, for the member-State to give preference to a unilateral and subsequent measure against a legal order accepted by them on a basis of reciprocity. . . . The pre-eminence of Community law is confirmed by Article 189 which prescribes that Community regulations have an "obligatory" value and are "directly applicable within each member-State." Such a provision . . . would be wholly ineffective if a member-State could unilaterally nullify its purpose by means of a Law contrary to Community dictates.[23]

Although hardly writing in the stirring and forceful rhetoric of John Marshall, the Court in this case, as Peter Hay points out, clearly applied a federal solution to "the classic supremacy problem of any two tiered federal legal system."[24]

Patterns of Litigation

It is clear that the judges in Luxembourg have provided channels amenable to federalizing tendencies, but to what extent are these channels being utilized? Any answer to this question is ultimately bound to become impressionistic. Good data are available, but what standards are we to use in determining just which patterns of litigation are consistent with the growth of a federal system?

In the analysis which follows, the Community will be tested against its own early record. The quantity and significance of Common Market litigation will be compared with the active

[10]

early days of the Coal and Steel Community. Of course, one must be cautious in drawing such comparisons. The tremendous scope of the Common Market means that its economic and political implications are far more portentous than those of the earlier organization. Moreover, the High Authority was charged with applying a largely self-executing treaty for coal and steel, while the E.E.C. Treaty was primarily a framework for working out common policy. Most of the Common Market crises have, therefore, not been amenable to litigation, since relatively few specific obligations are imposed by the Treaty. Cases in point include the negotiations for British entry into the Community and the development of a common agricultural policy.

Still, the Coal and Steel Community experience can be instructive so long as the limits of the comparison are kept in mind. What this experience suggests to me is that the role of litigation has been markedly curtailed in at least one important respect. During the formative years of the Coal and Steel Community, virtually all major controversies seemed to find their way to the judges in Luxembourg. In contrast, even when treaty obligations have been unambiguous, there has been little inclination to litigate the big Common Market problems. The partial Gaullist boycott of Community institutions in 1965 and 1966 is a good example, but undoubtedly there are others. I would, in short, agree with Andrew W. Green's observation: "Usually . . . the widely publicized controversies are not reflected in litigation before the Court of Justice." [25] Moreover, the European Community is a crisis-prone system — indeed, one that thrives on crises.[26] Litigation is then no longer part of crisis management; there is also reason to believe that its role in basic policy decisions is declining. General conclusions about this change will be developed below. At this point, let us simply note an apparent retreat from rule-of-law aspirations associated with the federalizing process.

This general impression tends to be borne out by a more systematic look at the volume of appeals to the Court of Justice since 1953 (Table 1). There has been considerable activity, distributed in a relatively uniform manner through the years, but there has not been much sign of the patterns that one might expect to emerge. Is it not, for example, surprising that the number of appeals rose only slightly after 1958, when the Common Market began to function? All other things being equal,

Table 1

APPEALS TO COURT OF JUSTICE OF THE EUROPEAN COMMUNITY
BY INSTITUTION

YEAR OF APPEAL	ECSC	EEC	EEC ARTICLE 177	TOTAL
1953	4			4
1954	8			8
1955	10			10
1956	9			9
1957	11			11
1958	40			40
1959	36			36
1960	20			20
1961	20	2	1	23
1962	14	14	5	33
1963	54	7	4	65
1964	9	10	6	25
1965	10	5	7	22
1966	4	20	1	25
1967 } 1968	8	26	32	66
1969	2	36	17	55
TOTAL	259	120	73	452

Source: Court of Justice of the European Communities, "Relevé Statistique 1953–1966," and "Statistiques Mensuelles," to July 1, 1970 (unpublished internal documents).

one might have expected that — given the striking difference in the scope of the two communities — Common Market figures would have dwarfed those of the Coal and Steel Community. Moreover, except for the inconclusive one-year increase registered in 1969, one does not see the upward trend in Common Market figures that might well have been expected as this framework treaty came to be implemented with binding rules. It should also be noted that litigation on the Coal and Steel Treaty has virtually ceased.[27]

The figures on government litigation (Tables 2 and 3) are also consistent with reservations about the federalizing implications of litigation. From the federal perspective, there is naturally a special significance to incorporating the governments into a

[12]

Table 2

SUITS BY MEMBER-STATES

	FRANCE	GERMANY	HOLLAND	BELGIUM	LUXEM-BOURG	ITALY	TOTAL
1953	1			1			2
1954	1		1			1	3
1955					1		1
1956	1					1	2
1957							0
1958	1	1					2
1959		1	1			1	3
1960							0
1961			1			1	2
1962		2					2
1963			1			1	2
1964				1		3	4
1965		2				1	3
1966		1	1				2
1967⎱ 1968⎰						1	1
1969	2	1				1	4
TOTAL	6	8	5	2	1	11	33

Sources: Court of Justice of the European Communities, "Relevé Statistique 1953–1966," and "Statistiques Mensuelles," to July 1, 1970 (unpublished internal documents).

pattern of constitutional coercion, since it is the independence of national units that must be curbed if an effective federal system is to be set up. The tables show that the governments participate regularly if not frequently as parties to suits involving the institutions of the Community.[28] Nonetheless, the figures do lend some credence to the argument that litigation is not really being used to compel member-states to accept Community norms. Of course, any appearance of a member-state before the Court of Justice could in itself be read as a concession to the rule of law. France under President de Gaulle seemed to take this position, during his term filing no suits at all. Generally speaking, however, the member-states have adopted a more flexible posture. They have been willing to appear before the Court of Justice and have even initiated litigation from time to time. But they have

Table 3

Suits Against Member-States
By Community Executive

	France	Germany	Holland	Belgium	Luxem-bourg	Italy	Total
1953							0
1954							0
1955							0
1956							0
1957							0
1958							0
1959							0
1960							0
1961		1				2	3
1962				1	1		2
1963				1	1	1	3
1964						1	1
1965	1						1
1966							0
1967 } 1968	1					2	3
1969	3			1		7	11
Total	5	1		3	2	13	24

Sources: Court of Justice of the European Communities, "Relevé Statistique 1953–1966," and "Statistiques Mensuelles," to July 1, 1970 (unpublished internal documents).

not taken advantage of the opportunity afforded by the Treaty to bring one another before the Court of Justice.[29] Moreover, the governments are more likely than are other parties to settle their suits out of court.[30] These tables are at best only suggestive but they seem to indicate that a rather flexible process of litigation is taking shape within a consensual framework of modified national choice.

Government litigation is sporadic and tangential to the great issues: it is also, I would argue, a sign of systemic weakness rather than strength. Political scientists have for a long time argued that the secret of successful joint action in the European Community is not to coerce compliance through constitutional

[14]

litigation but to mobilize a consensus through persuasive bargaining. It is not possible at this point to develop a detailed analysis of this intensely political process.[31] The process is, however, closely related to such things as executive initiative, the capacity to attract and satisfy relevant elites, and the ability to judge the priorities and urgent needs of the member-states. Litigation is, therefore, more a sign of breakdown than an index of Community authority. The record tends to support this judgment. Between 1958 and 1960, for example, the Coal and Steel Community was virtually overwhelmed by a coal crisis. The High Authority, unable either to persuade or coerce compliance with its program, simply did nothing. During this period of executive quiescence and general paralysis, it became common for dissatisfied governments and industrial firms to utilize litigation in an effort to prod the High Authority into meeting its responsibilities. There was, as I have written elsewhere, "an obvious tendency to thrust upon the Court the difficult jobs that the other institutions . . . failed to deal with in a satisfactory manner." [32] More recently, the comparatively large number of suits against member governments (Table 3) for failure to fulfill Treaty obligations may be taken as a'sign of the breakdown of Community bargaining procedures and a failure of executive leadership rather than of the federalizing process at work.

Federal forms in the shape of constitutional litigation may simply become prominent as the weakness of Community decision-making processes become clearer. It may, in other words, be a mistake, or at least premature, to look to rule-of-law models in gauging the progress of integration. As Judge Donner of the Court of Justice has pointed out:

> When the Common Market was instituted, all the legal scribes complained or rejoiced that this community was much less supra-national than the older one, the European Coal and Steel Community. And indeed in that first community the High Authority had a quasi-monopoly of power, the Council of Ministers intervening only to authorize certain of its decisions. But experience has shown the action of the more integrated Common Market to be far more powerful and effective.[33]

It is hardly surprising, then, that Mr. Justice Donner was not dissappointed to find that the governments have tended to resolve their controversies at the bargaining table — or even leave them unresolved — rather than resort to litigation. His approach to

[15]

these problems is conveyed well by the following comment on President de Gaulle's partial boycott:

> People have regretted that in last year's differences between France and its partners, the legal implications of the French absence in the Council was never submitted to the Court. That is much too legalistic an approach; it would have been the definite end of the communities as communities if the opposing parties had gone to law and asked a ruling on details that were no more than the juridical top of a political iceberg.[34]

All this does not mean that litigation does not play a part in the integrative process nor even that the federal prerogatives asserted by the Court serve no useful purposes. To understand the role of the Court of Justice better, let us now consider the manner in which the judges have dealt with the problems with which they have been presented.

Judicial Policymaking

The primary concern of this section will be with the impact of judicial decisions upon the substance of Community policy. Thus the focus will be on such policy problems as tariffs, antitrust, and social security rather than on the institutional channels considered in the previous section. To put it briefly, the record suggests that the judges have made only a rather modest contribution to the formulation of Community policy. The picture is not unambiguous: the policy activism of the judges seems to vary from situation to situation and is, admittedly, difficult to ascertain empirically. Let us look briefly at these problems of analysis before examining the work of the Court in some detail.

By and large, the Court of Justice has operated as a validator of decisions made by the Community executive rather than as a policymaker. According to Andrew Green, the Court has sustained the Commission and the High Authority in 107 out of 138 cases, or 78 percent of the time.[35] Since validation leaves the decisions of the executive intact, it has no ostensible impact on policy. But validation may also be indispensable to effective policymaking: it may, for example, enhance the legitimacy of Community rules or be vital to the policing of executive decisions. Validation could, in other words, have important longterm effects on the vigor of executive action and might even alter the direction of Community policy. Indirect consequences of this sort are, how-

[16]

ever, difficult to pin down or to verify.[36] For this reason, the following pages will be concerned with more direct and readily ascertainable effects.

Even by these standards, however, the work of the judges has had its policy consequences. After all, the judges have overruled the executive from time to time. Moreover, validating judgments have occasionally particularized the norm in question so as to make the meaning of Community policies more concrete and determinate.[37] But the most important channel for judicial policymaking has been the Court's active docket of Article 177 proceedings. Of course, in these cases validation is not really an issue since Community institutions are not parties to the basic litigation. In sum, when we consider the work of the judges in detail we shall see that the Court of Justice is making real if limited use of its opportunities to influence the development of Community policy.

At first glance, the Court's willingness to make policy contributions seems to vary at random, from situation to situation. Some patterns do emerge, however, if we think in terms of a matrix (Figure 1) which distinguishes suits by private parties from those by member-governments on one axis and direct appeals from Article 177 appeals on the other axis. The cells of the matrix certainly do not capture the full complexity of judicial behavior, but they do suggest significant distinctions. Direct

Figuro 1

POLICY MATRIX

		By Type	
		DIRECT	ARTICLE 177
By Party	Private		
	Governments		

[17]

appeals by private parties yield virtually no policy content, while private party litigation by way of Article 177 finds the Court occasionally playing a meaningful policy role. All the distinctions implied by the matrix may not be so persuasive, but this approach does provide some basis for generalization.

Direct Litigation. The limited policy impact of private party suits can be traced primarily to Article 173, which, it will be recalled, limits the appeal of a private party to "a decision addressed to him" or to decisions and regulations which are of "direct and specific concern to him." [38] Notice the crucial distinctions. There are acts which are individual both in form and in fact and may, therefore, be appealed. On the other hand, there are general norms addressed to member-governments and Community institutions, and individuals are not normally entitled to test these in court. Only when these general norms partake of some of the elements of an individual decision — that is, when they are of "direct and specific concern" to a private party — may they be tested in court.[39] It is, of course, clear that private parties may be influenced in a significant but indirect manner by general acts of the Community, but in such cases litigation is not permitted. The purpose of these limitations was to restrict, if not altogether foreclose, the opportunities of private parties to use litigation to challenge basic Community policies.

As implemented by the Court of Justice, the restrictive purposes of Article 173 seem to have been well served. In virtually all suits by business firms, the Court has used jurisdictional rules to avoid decisions of substance. In litigation bearing on the customs union, for example, the judges held that a German importer was not concerned "individually" by a decision even though he was one of a group of only thirty-five affected firms.[40] Similarly, the Court refused to consider the appeal of a Belgian exporter of a commodity because there were firms in other member-states exporting that product.[41]

There are, of course, some opportunities for individuals to seek judicial redress of their grievances. Some Coal and Steel litigation remains, and the Commission does occasionally address decisions directly to individuals. Antitrust actions often fall into this category and there are likely to be more and more of these actions in the future. Even when relief is granted in litigation involving individual decisions, however, the policy consequences tend to be rather limited, since the judgment is ordinarily based

[18]

on administrative irregularities. In one case, the Court declared that the Commission had improperly granted emergency protection to the German grain market since it had acted only to compensate for an administrative mistake by Community authorities.[42] Similarly, the Court annulled a Commission antitrust decision because the justification for the decision was not made sufficiently clear — thus leaving both the parties and the judges without the information necessary to determine its validity.[43] In the well-known Grundig case, which concerned the distribution of the firm's products in France, the Court granted partial relief from the Commission's decision. The judges even took the opportunity to consider the basic policy rationale for the Commission's prohibition of sole-agency agreements which entitle a single distributor to exclusive access to an entire national market — in this case France. The major thrust of the judgment was, however, to validate the reasoning of the Commission. Relief was granted only insofar as the Commission had annulled the entire distribution agreement rather than just the objectionable portions.[44]

An ancillary individualizing effect stems from the judicial interpretation of Article 175 of the Common Market Treaty, which purports to provide a remedy for the failure of the executive to act against some violation of the Treaty.[45] This provision has been construed by the Court of Justice to impose only the duty of response on the Commission. Apparently, any response will do and, therefore, the failure of the Commission to act is, in effect, unassailable.[46]

In contrast to private party litigation, suits by the governments can not be so easily diverted on procedural grounds. Consequently, underlying policy problems are ordinarily discussed in the judgments. The governments are no more likely, however, to win their suits than are private parties and the policy impact seems, therefore, to be quite limited. The customs union has provided the bulk of government litigation, particularly if one includes not just tariff problems but other provisions of the Treaty which are necessary to protect the integrity of the single market — controls on state subsidies, for example. Many of the suits concerned the manner in which exceptions were made to the general rules of internal free trade and also to the common external tariff. These were important matters, because the way in which exceptions were made could markedly alter the tone of

Community policy. The Commission could grant low rates or duty-free entry to a wide variety of goods under conditions specified in Article 25.[47] A free-trade gloss on third-country trade would, of course, have tended to alter the burdens and benefits of participation — reducing the incentives, for example, French farmers had for participating in the common agricultural policy.

In two suits involving Article 25, the German government challenged the Commission's refusal to provide special tariff quotas on low-priced wine used in the production of brandy and on *clémentines*, a succulent little tangerine eaten in Germany — particularly at Christmas.[48] Relief was granted by the Court in the wine case — but on a point of administrative procedure. The Court held that the Commission had failed to give adequate reasons for its decisions.[49] In both judgments, however, the Court validated the general lines of a Commission policy aimed at minimizing the exceptions to the common Community policy on third-country trade. In granting relief in the wine case, the judges made it abundantly clear that they saw the customs union as the bedrock of the Community.[50] What this means in practical terms was suggested by the ruling on clémentines, in which the judges gave their approval to the Commission's use of trade policy to change buying habits in favor of Community products. If clémentines were available only at a high price, it was reasonable for the Commission to assume that Germans would learn to enjoy the yuletide season with some other fruit. That is to say, the Court decided that it was perfectly proper for the Commission to take advantage of opportunities to promote the sale of apples or pears produced within the Community.[51]

These judgments might seem to imply judicial support for an autarchic trade policy. I would argue that they simply indicate judicial approval of wide Commission discretion. This interpretation is borne out by other judgments on related questions. Thus the Court turned back a challenge by the Italian government to a temporary Commission ban on imports of Italian refrigerators into France. Emergency action of this sort is authorized if such imports seriously threaten an economic "sector" or a "region."[52] The Commission action was taken to protect the small French refrigerator industry, which involved 11,000 workers and about 100 million dollars annually.[53] The Court held that the Commission was entitled to consider this an economic sector so long as it "is clearly distinguished from other related products."[54]

[20]

More recently, the Court stressed the discretionary powers of the Commission, under Article 80, to grant, withdraw, and/or refuse transportation subsidies.[55]

The judgments in these and other cases underscore the willingness of the judges to accept a system in which the Commission is endowed with broad discretionary powers. While discretion is obviously granted in the service of flexible market management, the possibilities of providing simple relief for administrative abuses are thereby reduced, since discretion and judicial control tend to work at cross-purposes to one another.[56]

This is not to suggest that the Court is, in fact, presiding over an arbitrary system which operates on the basis of administrative whim. The Commission has claimed all along for example that it used the emergency procedures of Articles 226 only in connection with a program for rationalizing production.[57] The *ad hoc* tendencies, in other words, stem directly from the Commission's determination to manage the market in the service of elusive goals like rationalization with minimal dislocation. Market management may just not yield to the application of anonymous norms to comparable situations and may better be left to the bargaining process than to judicial rulemaking.[58] Even in this loosely structured setting, however, the bargaining process itself seems capable of producing dependable if not anonymous norms. Figures published by the Commission indicate that only a small portion of the requests for special third-country quotas is rejected, but despite this fact the number of applications has been dropping steadily.[59] This implies that the parties have a reasonably accurate notion of what kinds of requests will be considered sympathetically by the Commission. Surely this notion must have emerged from the administrative procedure itself since the judgments of the Court of Justice are of no real help in this regard.[60]

Article 177 Proceedings. At first glance, the interlocutory judgments rendered under the provisions of Article 177 would seem unlikely to yield very much in the way of policy. Usually the Court of Justice has been called upon to provide the national courts with an interpretation of the E.E.C. Treaty. In these cases, *the national judges* are left with the job of applying that interpretation to the concrete situation posed in the litigation. Accordingly, the interstitial policymaking inherent in the job of norm particularization would also be passed on to the national tribunals. Therefore one might suspect that the Court of Justice would be a rather long step from substantive policy problems in Article 177 actions. For a number of reasons, this has not turned out to be the case, and the Court of Justice has probably had its greatest impact on substantive policy in such proceedings.

Let us begin by considering a few rather speculative points. In the first place, there is reason to expect that a particularly broad range of issues would be raised in Article 177 proceedings. So long as the Court continues to be flexible and receptive to all questions certified by national judges, private parties will be able to raise even the most explosive issues. There are no obvious boundaries. In the Costa case, for example, it was the refusal of an individual to pay his electric bill that led the Court of Justice to consider whether the nationalization of electric power in Italy was consistent with the Common Market Treaty. Another important point is that, in Article 177 proceedings, the Court of Justice is ordinarily the first Community organ to make a determination. The Court is not, therefore, in the delicate position of having to second-guess the Commission, as is usually the case in direct litigation. Indeed, the Court will in all likelihood be the first institution with expertise on Community matters to consider the problem. There is, therefore, no reason to perceive the active intervention of the judges as a threat to the authority of the Community, since its institutions are not pitted against one another. At the same time, the Court need not worry that it is intervening in the process of flexible market management. Finally, whatever the burden of intervention in Article 177 actions, responsibility for the outcome is inevitably shared with national judicial officials.

A careful look at Article 177 proceedings indicates, in addition, that the distinction between interpretation and application is in practice not as clear and precise as the two words suggest. The Court has certainly blurred the dividing line. In cases related to Community free trade, for example, the Court has gone well beyond mere interpretation.[61] In its judgments involving compensatory taxes levied on imports the Court stated that:

> The Court is not entitled by Article 177 of the Treaty to apply the rules of Community law to a particular internal tax, *but* it may interpret Article 20 of Regulation 19 with regard to the characteristics of an internal tax which is imposed on cereals originating in non-member States . . .[62]

In addition, if the Court is asked to consider an act of one of the

Community institutions rather than the Treaty itself, the judges are expected to interpret and consider "the validity" of those acts.[63] In assessing validity, the judges come still closer to application:

> 1. Examination of the question which the Finanzgericht, München, has put to the Court has not disclosed anything which affects the validity of the Commission's Regulation 144/65 of 18 October 1965.[64]

The tendency of the Court to move from the abstract to the concrete is comprehensible quite outside of leanings towards policy activism. The judges would understandably be concerned about the variations in Community law that could flow from unfettered discretion in application of abstract interpretive rulings by national tribunals. The national judges, themselves, may well be responsive to the call of uniformity and, given the abstruse and exotic quality of Community law, it is not surprising that national judges are willing to look to Luxembourg for guidance.[65] Even the Commission is sensitive to judicial leads in Article 177 proceedings — at least on matters relating to quantitative restrictions:

> The Commission is currently examining applications of these provisions in the light of certain new factors in the interpretation of the concept of charges with equivalent effect recently given by the Court of Justice.[66]

Clearly, the judges' opportunities to influence policy increase as the line between interpretation and application is blurred. It is less clear whether or when the judges are willing to take advantage of these opportunities. The policy value of the rulings discussed in the preceding paragraph should certainly not be exaggerated. The Court simply validated national taxes without suggesting much in the way of limits on what the governments had been doing. Moreover, there is little reason to believe that the Court of Justice is likely to become more activist when the policy stakes are high. Certainly, in the past the Court has, in my judgment, adhered strictly to the requirements that it interpret rather than apply in such cases. The Costa case, for example, involved the Court's most forthright declaration on the supremacy of Community law. But when we get beyond this vital structural question to the extremely sensitive policy issue of nationalization, we discover a detached interpretation which offers great leeway to the national judge. At about the same time, the Court skirted another rather delicate issue in a case which originated before an Italian court. This conflict involved restrictions on oil imports taken by the French government on behalf of its state monopoly.[67] These were, of course, early judgments and were handed down at a point when neither the primacy of Community law nor the acceptability of Article 177 could be taken for granted. It is more recently that the judges have begun to blur the distinction between interpretation and application. Still, given the record of the Court in general, there is no reason to believe that it is likely to allow itself to be intruded into intractable disputes in which fundamental policy matters are at stake. There remain, however, two important if not explosive areas in which the Court has utilized Article 177 opportunities in behalf of substantive results: social and antitrust policies.

Social policy is the only area in which the Article 177 proceedings seem actually to have altered the allocation of values. Social questions related to migratory workers have taken a major portion of the Court's attention — twenty-five out of ninety-two cases as of the end of 1969.[68] In these matters the judges in Luxembourg have been responsive to the claims of migratory workers and widows, who are often caught among national bureaucracies — each seemingly interested in minimizing the burdens on its resources. These cases illustrate the way in which Article 177 proceedings permit the Court to reallocate values without interfering with the Commission or altering Community policy. Indeed, with these problems of the migratory workers, the Court has simply accepted the burden for implementing a Community commitment to see to it that workers who move from country to country are not penalized. Nevertheless, the result of this litigation is to provide relief for people who would be in difficult straits if, for example, they received pension credit for only a portion of their working life.[69] Moreover, one senses a welcome change in tone in these judgments — that is, a willingness to cut through bureaucratic forms to the substance of the problem.

Antitrust problems can not really be considered at this point, but the Court's apparent willingness to play an interstitial policy role should be noted. First, it is important to realize how often Community antitrust law is relevant to litigation of business agreements in national courts. Since European antitrust law is by and large more stringent that national law, firms wishing to break an agreement that is no longer useful often plead Community

[24]

rules. Here the Court of Justice seems ready to seize the opportunity for stretching interpretation into application, as for example in a recent case involving the kind of distribution agreement which had been rejected in the Grundig decision. In the more recent case, the Court acknowledged that such arrangements are ordinarily contrary to Community law. But, after having looked closely at the facts, the judges suggested that the firms concerned were too small to affect intra-Community trade and should, therefore, be exempted from rules.[70]

Summary. Before going on to draw some general conclusions about the role of the Court of Justice within the Community system, let us recapitulate what we have learned about its judicial policymaking. First, it seems clear that any judicial policymaking that takes place, whether at the behest of private parties or governments, will be well beneath the level of high political issues. Just how far beneath high politics, it is difficult to specify but all evidence suggests rather modest policymaking on matters which are meaningful but not explosive. Certainly, the judges will be more circumspect than in the early Coal and Steel Community days, when all important matters found their way to the Court and were ordinarily treated by the judges in a forthright policy-conscious manner. In this connection, it should be noted that even the problems of social policy that have come to the Court have been in a sense peripheral. For example, Italian workers, who are responsible for the most significant movements within the Community, have not been involved in this litigation. Moreover, my interviews indicate that in the area of housing, where it was particularly difficult to gain compliance with Community regulations, the Commission has merely flirted with the idea of initiating litigation.

Secondly, the Court seems more inclined to exercise its modest impact on policy as part of Article 177 proceedings. As a result of the Court's stringent reading of Article 173, private parties are, of course, virtually excluded from influencing policymaking through direct litigation. But even government litigation seems not to result in any substantive rulings. Of course, this may all be a phase or it may have to do with the kind of problems that have been raised in Court. It is, for example, possible to envisage more vigorous judicial behavior in the antitrust area, where courts in general and the Court of Justice in particular have a history of active intervention both in terms of norm particularization and actual policymaking.[71] But in direct litigation the Court is always likely to be the prisoner of Commission expertise — a problem less likely to arise in Article 177 proceedings. Moreover, in these interlocutory judgments, the burden of judicial policymaking tends to fall ambiguously between the Court of Justice and the national judge, a situation which results in a sharing of responsibility and the possibility that the two courts can partake of one another's authority.

Conclusions

The picture that emerges is one of a court that has forcefully asserted federal prerogatives but has been very tentative on policy questions. In the Costa case, for example, the judges proclaimed the primacy of Community law but were reluctant to come to grips with the substance of the case — nationalization of the Italian electric industry. For the litigant, this inclination to avoid policy questions makes the judgment seem so much empty rhetoric and suggests a contrast between word and deed in judicial decisionmaking. The longer view is that the Court may be playing a constitutional rather than a policy role, and that we should judge the impact of the judicial process in procedural rather than substantive terms. Even if we admit, in other words, that the policy impact of the Court has been, at most, interstitial, it remains possible that the judges are shaping structural relationships between Community and national institutions.

The structural contributions of the Court are important and interesting but somewhat elusive. Certainly, the federal rhetoric can not be taken at face value, because the patterns of constitutional coercion and the hierarchical ordering of relationships associated with a federal system are not taking shape.[72] Instead, a more consensual neofunctional regime seems to be developing. Yet I do not mean to argue that the federal prerogatives are suffering from benign neglect or are beside the point. What is interesting is the way in which federal prerogatives are being put at the service of a neofunctional regime. A careful reconsideration of the record indicates how validation of executive authority and the increasing utilization of Article 177 contribute to the development of neofunctional relationships.

The consistent validation of executive authority might seem, at first glance, to be a step in the direction of federal ordering.

After all, in validating executive action in the face of challenges from both member-governments and interest groups, the Court does underscore the extent to which governments are bound by Community rules. Commission authority is, however, exercised in a consensual, nonfederal fashion. Ordinarily, the Commission acts only after a consensus has been molded through persuasive bargaining, technocratic expertise, and other neofunctional processes.[73] Government litigation is, in all likelihood, indicative of an objection to the manner in which the Commission is applying a Community rule. It should not, however, be taken as a fundamental challenge to the underlying consensus in any issue area. The record suggests that governments sufficiently disenchanted with the Community to reject any of its fundamental provisions would seldom be so indirect or legalistic as to use litigation to express such dissatisfactions.

The second way in which the Court has used federal prerogatives in the service of a consensual regime emerges from a consideration of the implications of the increasing number of Article 177 decisions. At the very least, these proceedings tend to incorporate an additional segment of national officialdom into the symbiotic process that is developing between the European and national systems. One can, in other words, perceive a legal parallel to the interpenetration of bureaucratic and political elites in the joint decisionmaking inherent in these interlocutory proceedings. Indeed, there is reason to believe that Article 177 may promote "deeper" interpenetration than ordinarily results from the political process, since lawsuits do not just engage elites but individuals and attorneys drawn from a variety of social strata and social roles. Finally, Article 177 litigation also involves relations among individuals in society; to the extent that these links are facilitated and promoted, litigation may become a significant agent of social community. Many would, of course, argue that this is the root function of law in any "liberal" system — that is, any system premised on a minimum of government intervention in economic matters. It is to these processes that we shall turn in the next section.

3. Interpenetration and the Consensual Regime

Introduction

Interpenetration has been a key concept in the study of regional integration virtually from the outset of research. Its importance stems from the belief that participation in regional decisionmaking processes will tend to socialize the participants and generate attitudes and behavior which are favorable to the regional system. As one study put it,

> We can well imagine how participants engaged in an intensive on-going decision-making process, which may extend over several years and bring them into frequent and close personal contact, and which engages them in a joint problem-solving and policy-generating exercise, might develop a special orientation to that process and to those inter-actions, especially if they are rewarding. They may come to value the system and their roles within it, either for itself or for the concrete rewards and benefits it has produced or that it promises.[74]

It is, of course, readily recognized that "participation could well increase enmity and reduce incentives for further collective action." [75] Researchers must, therefore, test for, rather than assume, positive results. Still, the evidence gathered so far suggests at least a net integrative effect which is positive.

But, if the net effect of actor socialization is believed to be

[28]

positive, the precise way in which such socialization alters attitudes and behavior is not really understood. It seems, however, to be an inertial kind of process which does not imply a transfer of loyalties nor even explicitly supportive attitudes towards the integrative undertaking. The assumption is that the habit of participation will lead national officials to "gradually internalize the Community's decisionmaking and bargaining norms . . . and thus accept the constraints upon nonconsensual action implied by those norms." [76] Similarly, it is believed that if interest group leaders, business firms, or individuals can be regularly engaged in regional processes, they will come as much by habit as by conscious choice to recognize and accept Community authority to deal with certain problems. Clearly such behavior increases the problemsolving capacities of the Community system regardless of whether the behavior is prompted by an attachment to the goals and methods of the European Community, per se. It is, of course, difficult to assess the staying power of socialization patterns, since we do not really know much about what it will take to reverse these inertial tendencies. But whether interpenetration is deemed cause or effect, if it can be identified with positive orientations and behavior it can be taken as an indicator of decisionmaking capacity.

In this section, I shall offer evidence which indicates that the legal processes of the Community are promoting both interpenetration and socialization. That is to say, I shall argue that these legal processes are promoting participation in the Community system and recognition of Community authority. The parallel with Community political processes is by no means perfect. Given the restricted number of participants in the Community's technocratic system, legal interaction probably involves a greater number of people but in a less intensive and more episodic fashion. Since socialization seems to be heavily dependent upon sustained and relatively intimate contact, the analysis I present can not be taken at face value. Moreover, this one study can not be expected to generate data quantitatively or qualitatively comparable to materials collected over the years by students of political integration. Consequently, what I am offering should be taken more as a hypothesis than a conclusion. However, the data are suggestive if not dispositive. They indicate that interpenetration, and with it a process at least comparable to socialization, seems to be taking place.

[29]

The essential question here is whether the national judges are being enlisted in the resolution of Community problems. While the term "enlisted" may seem a little odd at first glance it is really not at all unrealistic. Clearly, the judges on the Court of Justice have worked quite purposefully to promote the use of Article 177 procedures, which is the most unequivocal way in which national courts can participate in Community decision-making. As we have already seen, the judges have adopted a permissive attitude towards the rules prescribing the manner in which questions are to be sent forward. In addition, delegations of national judges have regularly been brought to Luxembourg to acquaint them with the Community, to foster a sense of participation and involvement, and, of course, to induce them to utilize Article 177. In 1969, for example, a total of 146 judges and other important officials of the high national courts and administrative tribunals was brought to Luxembourg.[77] These meetings offer what may be a partial surrogate for the more intensive interaction in the Council and in the working groups. While the interaction may not be so intense, the collaborative behavior required of the national judges by Article 177 proceedings is not as demanding as are crucial bargaining sessions in the Council.[78] In any case, let us consider the acceptance of Article 177 — first quantitatively and then qualitatively.

We have already seen that Article 177 decisions are becoming an increasingly important portion of the Court's docket. The remaining question is whether the procedure is being regularly utilized by national courts. Table 4 reflects the gradual upward trend in Article 177 opinions and it also indicates that courts from all the member states have been willing to utilize the procedure.[79]

The totals indicate a certain minimum of acceptance but the uneven distribution among the member-states raises some important questions. That is to say, given the consensual perspective, the important point is not occasional recognition of Community authority but habitual incorporation of national judges into the Community decisionmaking process. Using these standards, one is immediately struck by the enormous disparity between the opportunities national judges have had to utilize Article 177 and their actual utilization of the proceedings. By one count (Table 5), between 1958 and 1968 European Community legal questions

Table 4

ARTICLE 177 OPINIONS OF THE COURT OF JUSTICE
BY YEAR AND COUNTRY

	FRANCE	GERMANY	ITALY	HOLLAND	BELGIUM	LUXEM-BOURG	TOTAL
1962				1			1
1963				2			2
1964			1	5			6
1965		4	1	2			7
1966	1	1		2			4
1967	3	2		1	5	1	12
1968		11	1	2	1		15
1969 *	1	11			4	1	17

* 1969 figures are for suits filed rather than opinions delivered

Sources: Court of Justice of the European Communities, *Decisions Préjudicielles 1958–1968* (Luxembourg: Publications Office of the European Communities), 210 pp., and "Statistiques Mensuelles," to July 1, 1970 (internal document, unpublished).

Table 5

EUROPEAN COMMUNITY LITIGATION BEFORE NATIONAL COURTS

	HOLLAND	GERMANY	FRANCE	ITALY	BELGIUM	LUXEM-BOURG	TOTAL
1958	1	1					2
1959		4	2	1			7
1960	4	8		2		1	15
1961	6	3	3		3		15
1962	10	9	3	2	6		30
1963	9	20	8	3	3	1	44
1964	11	17	10	11	5		54
1965	5	22	9	1	6		43
1966	13	28	4	2	10		57
1967	12	33	8	5	12	1	71
1968	1	16	7	2	2		28
TOTAL	72	161	54	29	47	3	366

Note: The figures for 1968 are no doubt incomplete since reports of litigation in national courts are often not published until some time after the proceedings.

Source: A. W. Green, *Political Integration by Jurisprudence* (Leyden: A. W. Sythoff, 1969), pp. 610–655.

[31]

were considered in 364 actions before national courts. In the same period, the Court of Justice handed down fewer than 50 opinions (Table 4). Of course, these figures are not entirely satisfactory since only tribunals of last resort are required to seek interpretations from the Court of Justice; for others the Article 177 proceeding is a matter of discretion.[80] Figures for 1969 (Table 6) published by the Court of Justice suggest, however, that the proportion of cases referred by final jurisdictions is not by rough count much different from that of the lower courts.

What are the implications of this wide disparity between opportunity and utilization? According to Peter Hay:

> Article 177, if loyally employed by national courts, presents the Community Court with a far-reaching instrument for federalizing the relations between the Community and national legal systems.[81]

From all indications, Article 177 is not being loyally applied — at least not yet. What is more, if we take the admittedly rough indicators available it would seem that most of the member-states are *equally* reluctant to seize the opportunities of Article 177. But from a nonfederal point of view, the failure to use Article 177 is not in itself crucial if judges at various levels of the national judicial hierarchy are incorporating Community rules into their decisional processes. No doubt, as Professor Hay warns, the failure to utilize Article 177 consistently will result in discontinuities and ambiguities in Community rules. But if we are concerned less with uniformity than with participation, it is more important that Community norms are being regularly if flexibly implemented by national judges. In other words, the vital question is whether or not the refusal to use Article 177 amounts to a rejection of Community authority.

Clearly, quantitaitve analysis will not provide an answer to this question, which would probably vary some from court to court and country to country, in any case. It is, however, important to realize that there are a number of reasons why a national judge might decide against Article 177 proceedings without any intention of turning his back on Community norms or the Court of Justice. In the first place, national judges are supposed to utilize the procedure only when the litigation before them depends on the Community legal question,[82] and the recording procedure as I understand it makes no attempt to separate out such cases.[83] National courts might also not submit questions to

[32]

Table 6

ARTICLE 177: OPPORTUNITY AND UTILIZATION, 1969
BY NATION AND BY JURISDICTION

| | GERMANY | | BELGIUM | | FRANCE | |
	SUPREME *	OTHER	SUPREME	OTHER	SUPREME	OTHER
Community Law in National Litigation	16	36	3	6	3	3
Requests for Article 177 Interpretation	7	4	1	3	1	0

| | ITALY | | LUXEMBORG | | HOLLAND | |
	SUPREME	OTHER	SUPREME	OTHER	SUPREME	OTHER
Community Law in National Litigation	1	1	2	0	2	3
Requests for Article 177 Interpretation	0	0	1	0	0	0

* Based on compilations made in the documents below, supreme jurisdictions are presumably those "from whose decisions no appeal lies under municipal law" (Article 177, paragraph 3).

Sources: *Aperçu des travaux de la Cour de justice des Communautés européennes en 1969* (Luxembourg: Publications Office of the European Communities, 1970), p. 11, and "Statistiques Mensuelles," to July 1, 1970 (unpublished internal document).

the Court of Justice if the Court had already interpreted the provision in question, or if Article 177 proceedings would unduly delay the litigation.[84] Finally, it is possible that the national judge may simply decide that the issue is sufficiently clear to vitiate the need for reference to the Court of Justice. This position was expressly taken by the French Conseil d'Etat which utilized the *acte clair* doctrine and thus avoided use of Article 177.[85] However one may feel about the wisdom or motives of the Conseil d'Etat in this case or particular judgments in other cases, it is at least clear that the quantitative figures can not be taken at face value. With this caveat in mind let us attempt to determine, albeit tentatively, the extent to which national judges do seem to be accepting the authority of Community law.

The picture with respect to the recognition of the authority of the Court of Justice (Article 177) and the supremacy of Community law is a mixed one. "Acceptance," as Peter Hay points out, "has grown in recent years." [86] But he would undoubtedly agree with Richard Buxbaum's conclusion that, in most matters, there has been a real reluctance by national courts to use Article 177.[87] The problem seems to be most serious in France where the Conseil d'Etat gave lip service to its duty to apply Community law but was unwilling to use Article 177 until well into 1970.[88] On the other hand, the Cour de Cassation has referred two cases to the Court of Justice and has recognized the binding character of Community law.[89] In Germany the picture has been blurred by the decision of a German fiscal court holding that because the Community system operates outside the protections afforded by a separation of legislative and executive authority, it was contrary to the German constitution to transfer legislative power to Community institutions. After a delay of three and a half years, the German Constitutional Court was able to offer no more than an inconclusive opinion on the matter. In the interim, however, several other courts, including the Supreme Federal Fiscal Court, had concluded in favor of the constitutionality of the Treaty.[90] There would be no purpose served by a country-by-country look at the supremacy question since only in Holland can the primacy of Community law be taken for granted. Elsewhere, the status of Community law and the willingness to use Article 177 remain in doubt, although national judges seem increasingly receptive on both counts.[91]

Beyond recognition of the authority of the Court of Justice and acceptance of the supremacy of Community law, we must also ask whether or not national judges are willing to accept guidance on salient matters. This question has been posed in the Buxbaum article which focuses primarily on antitrust matters. He comes to the conclusion that the national judges send forward only the less important problems: "the more political and sensitive the issue, the more marked the divergence." [92] Professor Buxbaum's concern is, however, with utilization of Article 177 to develop a single regional antitrust policy. From this avowedly federal perspective, he finds the results disappointing. In my judgment, it is extremely unlikely that any kind of judicial review can promote an effective regional policy when national and Community policies are basically out of phase. The real question is whether the process is working out where there is a consensus on first principles. Is Article 177, in other words, capable of ironing out details and harmonizing conflicts over implementation? Professor Buxbaum's analysis is more hopeful from this perspective:

> In the administrative-law field, where the hard work of achieving local cooperation with Luxembourg's pronouncements is not with the tribunals that seek those prouncements but with the administrative agencies whose actions the certifying courts are there to control, the article 177 process has begun to take hold everywhere but in France.[93]

Any definitive conclusions on the progress of interpenetration and adaptation of national judges must await a more intensive and systematic analysis which would specify patterns and trends and test the impact of socialization.[94] Available data do, however, suggest that the process has begun and that the slope of the curve is generally upwards. It would, of course, be naive to ignore the reservations of Hay and Buxbaum and the obvious implications of the gap between opportunity and utilization of Article 177 proceedings. Clearly, there is resistance among national judges. But that resistance seems to be weakening and, as I have already argued, the needs of interpenetration are not so rigorous as those of the federalizing process. In other words, Article 177 is not as important as is regular utilization or application of Community law by national judges. The Commission, too, seems to recognize this:

> It is very desirable that use of the preliminary question procedure should continue to grow; but this does not mean, even for the highest courts, which are *required* to refer to the Court, that a judge must automatically submit a preliminary question every time one of the parties raises a point of interpretation of Community law. It is here that the very delicate question arises as to what is to be understood by an *"acte clair"* . . .

> There are perhaps better ways of ensuring that the procedure of Article 177 is fully effective. The Commission noted with great interest the suggestion made by the Parliament that Article 177 could be supplemented by the institution of an appeal procedure . . . such a procedure would enable the Community authorities to invoke the jurisdiction of the Court whenever they observed incompatibility between a decision of a domestic court and Community law.[95]

[35]

Beyond this issue of uniformity the important point is that the national judges are being incorporated into the Community system and thus increasing the Community decisionmaking capacity. At the same time, as the national judges adapt and apply Community norms in national litigation, attorneys are encouraged to rely upon these norms in pressing their claims. In this way, the reach and impact of the Community are extended further into the national systems. It is to the incorporation of attorneys and clients that we now turn.

Interpenetration: Attorneys and Clients

In order to assess the depth of interpenetration of Community legal processes, it is necessary to move beyond national judges to individuals and business firms. Given the broad and expanding thrust of the European Community, it is reasonable to believe that very large numbers of private parties will be touched in some way or another by Community rules and thus will be participating — consciously or unconsciously, willingly or reluctantly, continually or occasionally — in integrative processes. We must attempt to determine whether this participation is likely to lead to the kind of socializing experience which has been identified with involvement in Community political processes. That is to say, does participation in legal processes tend to legitimate Community institutions and norms and is it habit-forming?

The obvious way to assess the impact of Community legal processes on individuals and business firms is to conduct a series of interviews, but the legal public of the Community is so large and indeterminate that the sampling problem is all but insurmountable. Moreover, to pose questions about legal processes to laymen creates additional problems of question construction and evaluation. Accordingly, I decided to interview attorneys who had been involved with Community law, my assumption being that the attorneys could reasonably be perceived as the middlemen in a chain of interpenetration stretching from Community institutions to individuals.[96] Attorneys follow legal developments; react to them; transmit these reactions to their clients; and presumably influence client attitudes and behavior. While there is no way to determine how great an influence the

[36]

attorneys exercise over their clients, it is reasonable to infer some meaningful effects.[97]

My approach was prompted by a line of thinking developed by Talcott Parsons, who has contended that the attorney serves to "cool off" his clients and release tensions in conflictual situations.[98] Parsons' point has been succinctly summarized as follows:

> . . . the lawyer begins the necessary process by which an aggrieved citizen is made to cool down a little, to assess soberly the merits of his claim, the strength of his evidence, the possibility of another view, and the chance that after all his claim may not be worth pressing. The lawyer is trained to take the first shock of the client's indignation, in a manner which makes the client a little less bigotedly personal in his approach to a dispute.[99]

One might, in other words, take this to mean that, in the European Community, the attorneys would perform an adaptive or socializing function. Given the rather fluid and erratic character of the European Community system, another reasonable but contradictory hypothesis is also persuasive. It seems entirely plausible that attorneys would find this incipient legal system quite burdensome and that this could lead to considerable disaffection among the attorneys, which might in turn be transmitted to their clients. Were this to be the case, it could, of course, be argued that the legal processes would undermine the legitimacy of Community institutions and inhibit interpenetration — whatever other positive purposes might be served.

Before using the data on attorneys to determine which of the two notions makes the most sense, let us reflect for a moment on the stake in terms of individual involvement. We have already seen the available figures for national court litigation (Table 5), and it is therefore clear that we are talking about hundreds of firms and individuals. Moreover, this litigation seems to be increasing. In any case, litigation makes up only a small percentage of possible contacts between Community law and individuals and firms: Community antitrust law, for example, touches literally tens of thousands of business firms. While many of these contacts involve no more than filing a notification of agreements subject to Community norms, this notification procedure may be the first step leading to invalidation or modification of important business practices and must, therefore, be considered as more than simply *pro forma* contact with the Community. In addition, the Commission depends heavily on

[37]

Table 7

COMPARATIVE SATISFACTION OF ATTORNEYS
WITH
EUROPEAN COURT OF JUSTICE vs. NATIONAL COURTS
(Technical Considerations)
n = 59

	1a. Competence	1b. Result	2a. Consistency	2b. Clarity	3. Legality	4. General	Total
			(in percentages)				
Preference Euro. Court [a]	13	7	16	20	14	27	16
Preference National [a]	15	43	26	43	31	41	34
Total Preferences [a]	28	50	42	63	44	68	50
No Preferences [a]	73	50	58	37	55	32	5C
No Response	32	25	47	14	39	25	40

[a] Percentages are given in terms of those responding

1. Respondents were asked to compare the Court of Justice with higher courts in their own country with respect to:
   a. competence of the judges
   b. validity of the result
2. Respondents were asked to compare the judgments of the Court of Justice with judgments of national courts with respect to:
   a. consistency
   b. clarity
3. Respondents were asked to compare the willingness of the Court of Justice to defend the legal position against pressure from industrial and governmental pressures with the willingness of national courts.
4. Respondents were asked whether they would prefer to bring suit in the Court of Justice or in a national court.

complaints by business firms to uncover violations of the Community's antitrust provisions. In other words, the firms are responsible for a significant portion of the enforcement actions under Articles 85 and 86 of the Common Market Treaty.[100]

While it is difficult to be precise about the numbers, they are large and the parties are involved in a variety of significant ways.

The data suggest that the attorneys perceive differences between the Community and national systems, and that the national system is preferred virtually across the board, certainly in all direct comparisons. It is interesting, however, that the objections to the Court of Justice are not very strong (Table 7). When we add those who prefer the Court of Justice to those who are indifferent, we find that opposition to the Court of Justice is a minority position.

This finding is particularly interesting when it is put in perspective — that is, in terms of the attorneys' attitudes towards the general protection of individual rights and towards the bureaucracy (Table 8). Clearly, the attorneys do not see the

Table 8

COMPARATIVE SATISFACTION OF ATTORNEYS
WITH
EUROPEAN COMMUNITY vs. NATIONAL SYSTEM
n = 59

	1 ADMINISTRATIVE LEGALITY (in percentages)	2 PROTECTION OF THE INDIVIDUAL (in percentages)
Preference Eur. Com.[a]	11	14
Preference National [a]	68	59
Total Preference [a]	79	73
No Preference [a]	32	27
No Response	37	25

[a] Percentages are given in terms of those responding.

1. Respondents were asked to compare Community authorities with national authorities with respect to their disposition to accept legal arguments.
2. Respondents were asked to compare the national and Community systems in terms of the protections provided for individual interests.

[39]

Community as providing protection to individual rights comparable to that available in the member-states. Preference for Community processes is not markedly lower on these points, but among those responding there are fewer fencesitters. It would, in other words, appear that a small minority of attorneys is consistently favorable to the Community, but that most of the others see the Court of Justice, alone, in a reasonably favorable light (Tables 7 and 8).

It is important to realize, however, that the foregoing data deal only with comparative dissatisfaction. It is difficult to determine from them whether the attorney will work in the system willingly or grudgingly. Accordingly, a series of more direct inquiries concerning dissatisfaction were used. The responses tend to reinforce the initial impression of the acceptability of the Court of Justice. The attorneys seem to find the judgments of the Court of Justice sufficiently clear and consistent to enable them to work effectively with their clients (Table 9).

Table 9

SATISFACTION OF ATTORNEYS WITH PROTECTION OF INDIVIDUAL RIGHTS
n = 59

	1 SYSTEM IN GENERAL	2 LEGALITY IN ADMIN. PROCESS	3 ACCESS (ART. 177)	4 LAW vs. GOVERNMENT PRESSURE	5 LAW vs. INDUSTRIAL PRESSURE
			Court of Justice		
			(in percentages)		
Satisfaction [a]	42	46	49	63	92
Dissatisfaction [a]	58	54	51	37	8
No Response	19	56	37	12	14

[a] Percentages are given in terms of those responding

Respondents were asked:
1. Whether the legal system, considered as a whole, afforded adequate protection to individual interests.
2. Whether contacts with Community authorities showed them responsive to legal arguments.
3. Whether Article 177 provided sufficient access as an alternative to direct litigation.
4. Whether the Court of Justice was prepared to oppose any or all member-governments when the legal situation called for it.
5. Whether the Court of Justice was prepared to oppose the more powerful industrial interests when the legal situation called for it.

[40]

Table 10

SATISFACTION OF ATTORNEYS WITH COMMUNITY NORMS
(Technical Consideration)
n = 59

| | Court of Justice | | | COMMISSION | TREATY |
	1a. CONSISTENCY	1b. CLARITY	1c. CLARITY (ART. 177) (in percentages)	2a.	2b.
Satisfaction [a]	79	73	75	31	59
Dissatisfaction [a]	21	27	25	69	41
No response	42	14	46	24	37

[a] Percentages are given in terms of those responding

1. Respondents were asked whether the judgments of the Court of Justice were sufficiently consistent (a), clear (b) (c) to permit reliable guidance to clients.
2. Respondents were asked whether the Commission decisions (a) and the Treaty (b) permitted giving sufficiently definite advice to clients.

Beyond these technical questions, the attorneys feel that the Court is not likely to bend the law to satisfy either the member-governments or the more powerful industrial interests. The contrast with attitudes toward the Commission is very sharp. (Table 10). On the other hand, there is significant unhappiness with the protection afforded individual rights. But on these grounds, too, the Court of Justice comes off reasonably well when Article 177 proceedings are involved.[101]

In sum, these data reveal a rather puzzling pattern. Taken as a whole, the Community legal system is perceived as distinctly poorer than the national system. Still, the level of dissatisfaction, at least with the Court of Justice, is remarkably low. There would seem to be a marked willingness to use Community judicial processes. One can reasonably conclude that the Court of Justice seems to be nurturing an incipient sense of legitimacy among the attorneys. How can this be explained?

Again, the data provide at least part of the answer (Table 11). For the attorneys queried, Community legal business is not incidental. Many of them devote a substantial portion of their practice to Community problems and a significant number of them had joined a then new professional association concerned with emerging European law. Finally, it is clear that European

Table 11

PROFESSIONAL ENGAGEMENT OF ATTORNEYS IN EUROPEAN
COMMUNITY LEGAL PRACTICE

11–1. Proportion of Practice European

	ISOLATED CASES	5–10 %	10–33 %	33–60 %	61–100 %	No RESPONSE
Percentage [a]	20	28	19	24	9	8

11–2. Member of Association of European Jurists

	YES	No	No RESPONSE
Percentage [a]	42	58	10

11–3. Amount of Competition among Lawyers
for European Community Legal Problems

	VERY LITTLE	NORMAL	MORE THAN NORMAL	No RESPONSE
Percentage [a]	69	16	14	12

[a] Percentage figures for respondents are based on those responding

law is perceived as a speciality with a future in that there is relatively little competition in the field. There are, in other words, compelling reasons for the lawyers interviewed to make their peace with the Community rules: dissatisfaction, yes; disaffection, no! This is not to suggest completely cynical or self-serving motivations, for in many significant ways the attorney and his client have converging interests which inhibit disaffection for both of them.

To explain the point better, let us consider the client's perspective. First, he is likely to learn from the attorney whether he has any obligations to the Community. It is not unreasonable to assume that, particularly in the antitrust field, the Community will first become personally meaningful when he is informed by his attorney that certain business agreements have become subject to Community regulations. For a businessman in Germany, for example, this will mean at the most some additional rules with which he must comply. In Italy, on the other hand, it may mean his first contact with antitrust law. Where experience with antitrust law is minimal or nonexistent, the attorney can play a significant role in conveying to his client a sense of its legitimacy.

In addition to confronting the client with his obligations, the attorney will also convey a notion of the protection afforded by the Treaty. It is important to realize that regardless of how poor the protection afforded by the Community system may be, it still in many cases represents another option for the client — another way of getting results or affecting events. We saw, for example, that in the antitrust area Community law provided the attorney with additional legal arguments for extricating his client from a collusive agreement that no longer served its purpose. There is, however, a still more fundamental point which helps to explain why attorneys are not necessarily disturbed by the technical shortcomings of the system — clarity, consistency, etc. The fact is that to a very important extent it is the ambiguities of the law that make the system bearable. A large portion of the service that the attorney performs is helping his client manipulate these ambiguities. Time and again, I found that attorneys took this general posture towards imperfections in the Community system. It is for this reason, incidentally, that I am less concerned than others about the failure to adhere strictly to the provisions of Article 177.

In any case, the attorney helps the client to learn where he stands in the Community system — what channels of influence are open to him, how strictly rules are enforced, what rights are guaranteed.[102] It is also important to realize that the attorney and his client have converging goals; they are both result-oriented. The attorney can, in other words, be expected to identify his immediate interests with those of his client. For all these reasons, the attorney is likely to have considerable influence over the attitudes and behavior of his clients with respect to the European Community.

There is, however, a subtle but important distinction between the attorney's position and that of his client. The attorney may work to optimize his client's position and to minimize the client's obligation, but the attorney has a stake in the Community system which is partially independent of the client relationship. If the client does not feel a minimal sense of obligation for Community norms, the attorney is without a job. Whether the attorney is predisposed towards compliance or evasion, if there are no rules to obey there are no rules to manipulate. Moreover, to work effectively within a system, the attorney must be constantly aware of the longrange impact of his behavior. A reputation as a troublemaker is likely to prove counterproductive and while some attorneys seemed aware of and even pleased by such reputations, most seemed more inclined to play the game.[103]

In sum, I am simply suggesting that in the Community setting, where legitimacy is not well established, the legal profession is likely to foster and nurture respect for Community norms and perhaps for the regime. So far as the attorney is concerned, the process is likely to be almost involuntary — particularly once he has some kind of professional stake in Community legal business.[104] Some attorneys are attracted because they are committed to European integration; others simply stumble into an occasional case and agree to handle it.[105] I would suspect there will be an increasing "Community bar," with lawyers attracted to this speciality for the same combination of reasons that leads others elsewhere. Courses on European law are being offered at European universities and in 1969 alone more than five hundred students visited the Court of Justice.[106] Exactly how this process starts, it is difficult to say except to argue, in somewhat circular fashion, that lawyers will respond to a system of rules which appears to be authoritative. But what makes it appear authoritative? Again, we can only guess, but it would seem that the assertion of federal prerogatives by the Court of Justice in Luxembourg with the attendant national publicity helps, as does the kind of partial deference national courts are beginning to offer to Community rules and institutions. More prosaically, it is no doubt significant that thirty-seven legal journals — only a small portion of them European law journals, as such — now report Community legal developments.[107] In other words, to the extent to which Community institutions seem reasonably like other institutions at the national level, it is clear that the lawyer's skills will be useful.

The attorney data presented so far take us one step, but just one step, beyond the initial "participation" argument. That is to say, not only does it seem likely that the legal process elicits participation, it also seems likely that the attorneys tend to engender among their clients a sense of the procedural legitimacy of supranational institutions, in general, and of judicial institutions, in particular. We still have not learned anything, however, about the actual kinds of behavior that the attorney is likely to foster. Obviously, this is a crucial question in estimating whether this participation is likely to work to alleviate stress.

To be somewhat more specific, we might want to ask the following kinds of questions about the behavior of the business-man: Will he conform to the rules or seek to evade them? Will he resort to litigation or will he bargain? If he decides to bargain, will he turn directly to Community authority or will he seek to work through the national bureaucracy? In part, these decisions will depend on the manner in which the attorney portrays the Community and in part on the attorney's idea of the law. Some of my data bear on this latter question.

As Table 12 indicates, each of the attorneys was asked to rank order six functions of the Court of Justice and the legal system of the Community according to importance.

Analysis of the answers suggests that these lawyers are likely to exert a functional and rather noncontentious influence on the system. Notice the disinclination to use the law for political purposes, i.e., to control the actions of the member-states. Even the conflict-resolution function which would suggest litigation ranks rather low — except perhaps among the Germans. Notice

Table 12

PERCEIVED ROLE OF LAW

n = 35

		ALL	HOLLAND	GERMANY	FRANCE
I.	Clarifying the operational meaning of the Treaty	1	1	1	5
II.	Resolving conflict	4	4	3	4
III.	Increasing the stability of the Community	5	5	5	3
IV.	Providing workable solutions to Community problems	3	3	4	2
V.	Limiting the influence of the larger states	6	6	6	6
VI.	Making certain that Community operations conform to the Treaty	2	2	2	1

Note: The results presented were derived by application of White's Rank Order Correlation Coefficient and all were of either 1 or 5 percent significance according to a Chi-Square test. The results in Belgium and Italy were not significant and have therefore been excluded.

Seven of the forty-two attorneys questioned in the above three countries failed to respond. No response rate = 17 percent.

[45]

the rather high priority given to making certain that Community operations conform to the Treaty. This I would suggest is evidence of the kind of formalism that seems to characterize the European bar — the response could be deemed virtually a reflex. Of course, if it were combined with litigious inclinations, one might expect considerable conflict. However, note also the strong consensus on the communication theme which is inherent in the notion of "clarifying the operational meaning of the Treaty" and the reasonably strong preference for "workable solutions."

Conclusion

The information presented in this section does seem to reveal the beginnings of consensual processes crystallizing within and around the legal system. Certainly, the bar tends in the nature of things to be rather easily coopted and, in the absence of other sources of advice on Community legal problems, it is reasonable to infer that the client will be influenced by his attorney. Moreover, there is strong reason to suspect that the attorney will seek to function in part as a mediator between his client and the Community system — helping all participants in a dispute to see their problems in the broader context of social relations from which Community rules derive. Even in pressing claims based on Community law in national courts, the attorney is reinforcing from below the call of the Court of Justice for active implementation of the procedures of Article 177. The judges for their part are beginning to respond to a variety of pressures and inducements by incorporating Community rules into their decisional processes. Of course, this development is somewhat erratic and the application of Community norms far from uniform. I would argue, however, that it is just this course of events which is likely to promote consensual patterns — that is to say, a process which softens rather than sharpens the hard edges of Community rules and thus makes them more palatable to all participants. Certainly, the inclination of national judges is to court ambiguity in the use of Article 177, and we have also seen that lacunae in the system are seen more as opportunities than as handicaps by the attorneys. In short, this is a process which can not be caught up by research paradigms which focus exclusively on federalizers or on the perfection of legal machinery.

4. The Role of Law?

In making final assessments, it is necessary to recall and consider the gap between the assertive rhetoric of the Court of Justice and the modest role the judges have played in the policy process. Except for a brief period in the life of the Coal and Steel Community, there is little, if any, evidence that the Court has contributed directly to the Community's capacity to impose "constitutional" solutions on difficult problems. The judges may have imparted some legitimacy to efforts by the Commission to mobilize a consensus or to deal with certain limited kinds of deviant behavior. The judges may have authorized enforcement action by the Commission against member-governments that resisted the application of various Community rules and they have handled other cases with significant implications for large numbers of people. The assertion of federal prerogatives may even be among the preconditions to the process of legal interpenetration that was discussed in the last section. Nonetheless, the judges do not appear to have been very active federalizers, and the most important controversies are seldom litigated.

It is in this light that we must make our assessment of the meaning and implications of legal interpenetration — even if that process is largely independent of federal prerogatives. It is true that the attorney data seem to complement and to add new dimensions to what we know about Article 177 proceedings and litigation in national courts. These data provide further evidence of interpenetration and also reveal additional ways in which

[47]

Community rules can be brought into the mainstream of national life. It is true, in addition, that this process would seem to have expansive and self-sustaining tendencies stemming from the normal professional motivations of attorneys, the self-interest of clients, and to some extent the craftsmanlike habits of judges. Thus, while the process is perhaps initiated by the assertion of federal prerogatives, these coercive tendencies seem to fade into the background so that on a day-to-day basis deference to authority becomes a given rather than a primary factor in the functioning of the system. The problem in all of this is that the legal process remains at the margins of basic public policy and therefore suspect as a potential integrator.

The legal process may be engaging ever larger numbers of private citizens and judicial officials, but one is left with real questions about the quality of the transactions that are identified with interpenetration. For all its participants, the legal process is so purposefully depersonalized that one can not be at all sure that the sense of participation in a common undertaking, which is the hallmark of socialization, ever really becomes operative. In addition, the expansive tendencies are directly related to pro-fessional rather than political concerns. The numbers may, in other words, be large and the process may be penetrating deeply into the society, but is this engagement politically significant? Does the habitual use of and deference to Community institutions and rules tend to build up support for the Community? And what about the social implications of this legal web? To what extent are these legal linkages feeding the incipient transnational society? In sum, regardless of numbers, if the process is politically and socially trivial, ephemeral, or easily reversible, the Com-munity stake in legal integration may not be very high. These questions are raised but certainly not answered by this paper which is, therefore, at best a beginning.

FOOTNOTES

1. There are, strictly speaking, three communities: the European Coal and Steel Community which began to function in 1952, the European Economic Community (The Common Market), and the European Atomic Energy Community (Euratom), both of which commenced operations in 1958. While based on separate treaties, the three organizations share common institutions including the Court of Justice, the Executive Commission, the Parliament, and in most respects the Council of Ministers. Consequently, I shall refer to the European Community in this paper although some might consider this characterization imprecise or perhaps premature. For a discussion of the institutional structures and patterns of authority, see Leon N. Lindberg and Stuart A. Scheingold, *Europe's Would-Be Polity: Patterns of Change in the European Community* (Englewood Cliffs, N.J.: Prentice-Hall, 1970), pp. 82–100.

2. Legal writing often seems abstract and formalistic to the layman, but it is actually an intensely practical enterprise. The resourceful lawyer who understands the multiple implications and possible variations of a judgment or of some other Community norm can be exceedingly useful to his client. Thus, the writer who explores these legal implications and variations is participating, albeit indirectly and vicariously, in the multitude of discrete transactions which are the ongoing business of the European Community.

3. In arguing against the idea of the Court of Justice as a federalizer, this paper is probably in tune with the civil law perspective. My position, however, stems from an understanding of the Community political system rather than from any preconceived ideas about judicial activism. Moreover, in most other respects this paper, will no doubt, not be in tune with the approach of continental lawyers.

4. For those interested in legal problems as such, *The Common Market Law Review* regularly offers an annotated bibliographic essay as well as its own contributions to understanding the development of Community law.

5. While most of the work of the European Community is carried out in Brussels, the European Parliament meets in Strasbourg and the seat of the Court is in Luxembourg. Luxembourg also houses most of the Community's statistical offices and is host to a portion of the meetings of the Council of Ministers.

6. The principal officials of the Court of Justice are the seven judges, two advocates general, and a chief clerk. For a discussion of these positions as well as a detailed assessment of a major portion of the

[49]

Court's work, see Stuart A. Scheingold, *The Rule of Law in European Integration* (New Haven, Conn.: Yale University Press, 1965).

7. This distinction between structure and policy seems to catch up most of the important problems and will, I believe, disclose some significant variations in the emerging patterns.

8. The data on national courts and on litigation before the Court of Justice were readily available and had only to be collected, in some cases from unpublished sources, and analyzed. Learning about the reactions of attorneys who participate in the Community system required extensive interviewing since information is not otherwise available.

9. Andrew Wilson Green, *Political Integration by Jurisprudence* (Leyden: A. W. Sythoff, 1969), p. 1. The meaning and implication of these categories, although not Green's study itself, will be considered in the second section of this paper.

10. Andrew Wilson Green, *Political Integration by Jurisprudence*; Peter Hay, *Federalism and Supranational Organizations* (Urbana, Ill.: University of Illinois Press, 1966); W. Andrew Axline, *European Community Law and Organizational Development* (Dobbs Ferry, New York: Oceana Publications, Inc., 1968); and Werner Feld, *The Court of Justice of the European Community* (The Hague: M. Nijhoff, 1963). Among the numerous articles, see, particularly, Stefan A. Riesenfeld and Richard M. Buxbaum, "N.V. Algemene Transport-en Expeditie Onderneming Van Gend & Loos c. Administration Fiscale Neerlandaise: A Pioneering Decision of the Court of Justice of the European Communities," *The American Journal of International Law*, Vol. 58, No. 1 (January 1964), p. 152, and Eric Stein, "Toward Supremacy of Treaty-Constitution by Judicial Fiat: On the Margin of the *Costa* Case," *Michigan Law Review*, Vol. 63 (1965), pp. 491–518.

11. See particularly Articles 33 and 35 of the *Treaty Establishing the European Coal and Steel Community* (hereinafter cited as E.C.S.C. Treaty). All E.C.S.C. Treaty citations are taken from the English translation published by the High Authority and printed in London.

12. This oversimplified explanation should be modified at least to indicate that there are restrictions on the conditions for bringing suit even when a firm's interests are clearly at stake and that suits can be brought against other enterprises and member-governments only in an indirect fashion — that is, in an action against the High Authority for its failure to take whatever steps were necessary to bring the behavior of the state or the firm into line with the Treaty. For a more systematic explanation, see Stuart A. Scheingold, *The Rule of Law*, pp. 41–48.

13. Article 173, second paragraph: "Any natural or legal person may . . . appeal . . . against a decision which although in the form of a regulation or a decision addressed to another person, is of *direct and specific* concern to him." (Italics added). *Treaty Establishing the European Economic Community* (hereinafter cited as E.E.C. Treaty. All E.E.C.

Treaty citations are taken from the English translation published by E.E.C. Commission, as document 1931bis/5/57/4.

14. 25/62 Plaumann & Co. v. The E.E.C. Commission — 3 *Common Market Law Reports* 29 — decided 15 July 63 — (hereinafter cited at 3 *C.M.L.R.* 29). For a discussion of the Coal and Steel Community retreat, see Scheingold, *The Rule of Law*, Chapter 10.

15. According to Article 177, paragraphs 2 and 3, any national court judge *may* seek interpretations from the Court of Justice if he feels that judgment "depends on a preliminary decision" on Community legal questions. Courts of last resort are *required* to refer Community legal questions to the Court of Justice.

16. 75/63 Unger v. Bestuur der Bedrijfsvereniging voor Detailhandel en Ambachten, 3 *C.M.L.R.* 319, 322 — 19 March 64. This same point is made in the *Third General Report on the Activities of the Communities 1969* (Brussels-Luxembourg: 1970), p. 456: "In the same spirit, the Court maintained its very liberal approach in the matter of admissibility. For instance, it recognizes the admissibility of a preliminary question raised in a summary procedure. Nor will it refuse to entertain preliminary questions because they are imperfectly worded."

17. 13/68 Salgoil S.p.A. v. Foreign Trade Ministry of the Italian Republic, 8 *C.M.L.R.* 181, 193 — 19 December 68.

18. It is interesting to note that this "liberal" approach to Article 177 rests firmly on a "conservative" base — respect for the determinations of national judges in national litigation. The general thrust of this posture is to insure maximum independence of national and Community legal systems. Only with respect to Treaty matters are the systems in any sense integrated.

19. 26/62 N.V. Algemene Transport-en Expeditie Onderneming van Gend en Loos v. Nederlandse Tariefcommissie, 2 *C.M.L.R.* 105, 129 — 5 February 63. For an early commentary on the details and implications of this case, see Riesenfeld and Buxbaum, "N.V. Algemene. . . ."

20. 7, 13, 20, 25, 27, 28 & 31/67 Molkerei-Zentrale Westfalen/Lippe GmbH *et al.* v. Hauptzollamt Paderborn *et al.*, 7 *C.M.L.R.* 187, 194 — 3 and 4 April 68.

21. According to Article 36 of the E.E.C. Treaty, governments remain entitled to act in defense of "public morality, public order, public safety, the protection of human or animal life or health," etc.

22. According to Article 226 of the E.E.C. Treaty, the Commission may authorize measures of safeguard or adaptation which are contrary to the Treaty in order to deal with serious problems in an economic sector or region. Article 235 empowers the Council on proposal of the Commission, and following consultation with the Assembly, to enact any measure not otherwise provided for, which is necessary to "achieve . . . one of the aims of the Treaty." For related case law, see particularly 7/61 Re Quantitative Restrictions on Imports of Pork

Products into Italy: Commission of the E.E.C. v. The Italian Government, 1 *C.M.L.R.* 39, 56 — 19 December 61.

More recently, the Court took a similar position with respect to protective actions undertaken by France in the wake of the 1968 general strike, 6 & 11/69 E.E.C. Commission v. France: Re Export Credits, 9 *C.M.L.R.* 43, 64–65 — 10 December 69.

23. 6/64 Costa v. Ente Nazionale per l'energia Elettrica (ENEL), 3 *C.M.L.R.* 425, 455–456 — 15 July 64. For a full consideration of the details and implications of this interesting case, see Eric Stein, "Toward Supremacy. . . ."

24. Peter Hay, "The Building of the European Economic Community and its Restrictive Practice Laws," (unpublished manuscript), p. 42.

25. Green, *Political Integration*, p. 444.

26. For an incisive discussion of crises in integrative systems, see Philippe Schmitter, "A Revised Theory of Regional Integration," *International Organization*, Vol. 24, No. 4 (Autumn 1970), pp. 842–844.

27. The decline in Coal and Steel litigative activity is masked by a plethora of litigation relating to an early period and involving questions of administrative regularity in a scrap subsidy scheme. (For details, see Scheingold, *The Rule of Law*, Chapter 6.) If scrap cases are excluded there has not been a year with more than four or five appeals since 1960.

28. The tables are not an altogether accurate portrayal of the judicial involvement of member-governments. Article 177 actions are not included, nor are cases in which the governments were not formally parties although they may have been involved in the dispute that gave rise to the litigation or may even have submitted briefs to the Court of Justice. See Green, *Political Integration*, Chapter 8.

29. "Any Member State which considers that another Member State has failed to fulfill any of its obligations under this Treaty may refer the matter to the Court of Justice." Article 170, paragraph 1, E.E.C. Treaty. See also Article 89, E.E.C. Treaty.

30. Of the thirty-eight suits involving governments that were filed between 1953 and 1966, just over 35 percent were withdrawn before a decision could be rendered. Only about 20 percent of the total number of suits filed during this period were settled out of court. There is nothing unusual about bargained settlements of litigation; they occur regularly in most judicial systems for a variety of reasons. It is, then, only the greater inclination of governments to settle out of court that is noteworthy — and even this only in the general context of governmental reluctance to litigate. These figures were compiled from "Relevé Statistique 1953–1966," an unpublished document prepared at the Court of Justice. For a discussion of the role of out-of-court settlements in the Coal and Steel Community, see Scheingold, *The Rule of Law*, pp. 301–308.

31. See Leon N. Lindberg and Stuart A. Scheingold, *Europe's Would-Be Polity*.

32. Scheingold, *The Rule of Law*, pp. 272–273.

33. A. M. Donner, *The Role of the Lawyer in the European Communities* (Evanston, Ill.: Northwestern University Press, 1968), p. 14.
34. *Ibid.*, p. 62.
35. Green, *Political Integration*, p. 223. The pattern does not vary much for the two executives: the High Authority has won 88 out of 114 suits and the Commission 19 of 24. *Ibid.*, p. 503.
36. Green is particularly sensitive to the weakness of the usual international secretariat and correspondingly appreciative of the validating powers of the Court of Justice: "With a judiciary an administration can make policies within the limits of its competence with an assurance that its policies are likely to be observed by member states, because the judiciary will assure maintenance of its policies in the face of disputes among member states as to what the policy is or ought to be . . . The Court of Justice has given the High Authority and the E.E.C. Commission such support in the face of opposition by member states . . ." *Ibid.*, p. 222. Dr. Green's certitude that validation will assure policy implementation can be traced to the logic of the federal perspective. He provides us with no evidence in support of his position, however.
37. This process of norm particularization tends to be inherent in the application of general rules to specific situations. Of course, the judges can if they wish frame their decisions so as to offer only limited guidance of this sort. On the "open texture" of rules, see H. L. A. Hart, *The Concept of Law* (London: Oxford University Press, 1961), pp. 121–132.
38. *Supra*, pp. 7–9.
39. Article 189 of the E.E.C. Treaty specifies and explains the three binding acts that may be adopted by the Council and the Commission — regulations, directives, and decisions. Nonbinding recommendations and opinions may also be issued.
40. 25/62 Plaumann & Co. v. The E.E.C. Commission, 3 *C.M.L.R.* 29, 47 — 15 July 63. The Court also rejected a suit against a Council of Ministers regulation on grounds that indicate that regulations are automatically exempt from suits by private parties. 6/68 Zuckerfabrik Watenstedt GmbH v. E.C. Council, 8 *C.M.L.R.* 26, 36–37 — 11 July 68. It is of course true that Article 173 only permits suits against decisions, but in an analogous problem in the Coal and Steel Community, the Court looked behind the form to the reality of the decision. As one commentator put it: "The Court has so far interpreted an individual act rather liberally to the detriment of a general act so as to ensure the widest possible protection of individuals." Gerhard Bebr, *Judicial Control of the European Communities* (New York: Praeger, 1962), p. 42.
41. 1/64 Glucoseries Réunies v. E.E.C. Commission, 3 *C.M.L.R.* 596, 603 — 2 July 64.
42. 106 & 107/63 Alfred Toepfer KG and Getreide-Import Gesellschaft GmbH v. E.E.C. Commission, 5 *C.M.L.R.* 111, 144 — 1 July 65. See also the follow-up case concerning damages resulting from the Com-

mission's mistake, 30/66 Firma Kurt A. Becher v. Commission of the European Communities, 7 *C.M.L.R.* 169 — 30 November 67.

43. 8–11/66 Re Noordwijka Cement Accord, 6 *C.M.L.R.* 77, 105 — 15 March 67. Article 190 specifies that: "The regulations, directives, and decisions of the Council and the Commission shall be supported by reasons . . ."

44. 56 & 58/64 Établissements Consten S.A. and Grundig-Verkaufs-GmbH v. E.E.C. Commission, 5 *C.M.L.R.* 418, 474–475 — 13 July 66.

45. Article 175 of the E.E.C. Treaty empowers a private party to complain to the Court of Justice should the Council or the Commission fail "to address to him" certain acts required by the Treaty. Litigation is authorized, however, only if the Council or the Commission is first invited to act and "has not stated its attitude" within two months.

46. 48/65 Alfons Lütticke GmbH *et al.* v. E.E.C. Commission, 5 *C.M.L.R.* 378, 387 — 1 March 66. Again, the contrast with the Coal and Steel Community is instructive, since the comparable provision (Article 35 of the E.C.S.C. Treaty) was used very effectively to prod the High Authority. Scheingold, *The Rule of Law*, pp. 41–43. In these cases, the Court regularly decided whether or not the High Authority had actually violated the Treaty. In other words, the Court actually evaluated the High Authority's explanation of its failure to act according to the relevant provisions of the Treaty.

47. By and large, Article 25 permits exceptions to normal import duties on products coming from third countries if conditions of supply and demand warrant a temporary lowering of trade barriers. This article is linked to a series of itemized product lists annexed to the E.E.C. Treaty. For some products exceptions may be authorized by the Commission alone; for others the Commission must act together with the Council.

48. Wine falls into a category of products for which the Commission *must* reduce or eliminate the tariff burden when the market cannot supply the necessary quantities, i.e., where "harmful consequences for some processing industries" will result. For the clémentines, on the other hand, the Commission *may* grant exceptions if the imports would not result in a "serious disturbance" of the market. (See E.E.C. Treaty, Article 25, sections 2 and 3, respectively.)

49. 24/62 Re Tariff Quota on Wine: German Federal Republic v. Commission of the E.E.C., 2 *C.M.L.R.* 347, 367–368 — 4 July 63.

50. *Ibid.*, p. 366.

51. 34/62 Re Import Duties on Sweet Oranges: German Federal Republic v. E.E.C. Commission, 2 *C.M.L.R.* 369, 393–394 — 15 July 63.

52. Article 226, Section 1, E.E.C. Treaty, *supra*, fn. 22. This article ceased to apply at the end of the transitional period (31 December 1969).

53. 13/63 Re Electric Refrigerators: The Italian Government v. E.E.C. Commission, 2 *C.M.L.R.* 289, 296 — 17 July 63 (submissions of Advocate General Lagrange — 28 May 63).

54. *Ibid.*, p. 310.

55. 1/69 Re Preferential Freight Rates: Italy v. E.E.C. Commission, 9

C.M.L.R. 17, 28 — 9 July 69. The Commission is directed by Article 80 of the E.E.C. Treaty to alter rate schedules which amount to carrier subsidies while being receptive to the use of special rates to promote regional economic development and planning.

56. Such is the clear implication of the Italian transport case. If the Commission is entitled to take into account a greater number of unspecified conditions in making subsidy decisions, the requirement that the Commission give reasons for its decision loses most of its purpose, since there are no standards for assessing the propriety of the reasons. This was the complaint of the Italian government and the Court did little in its judgment to allay such fears. It should, of course, be recalled that this requirement for a reasoned decision is the most frequent basis for granting relief and maintaining the administrative integrity of the Commission position.

57. E.E.C. Commission, *Seventh General Report (1964)*, pp. 44–65.

58. One of the conclusions which the Commission drew approvingly from the refrigerator judgment was: "Differential treatment among the Member States need not automatically imply discrimination where the situations concerned are not comparable; as the Commission is required under Article 226 to restrict intervention to the minimum that is absolutely necessary, it ought to be free to take action only against the root cause of the difficulties." *Ibid.*, p. 44.

59. Over the five years between 1961 and 1965 only about 17 percent of the requests based on Article 25, paragraph 3, were rejected. E.E.C. Commission, *Tenth General Report, 1966*, pp. 68–69. See also European Commission, *Second General Report on the Activities of the Community 1968* (Brussels-Luxembourg: Publications Department of the European Communities, 1969), p. 23.

60. The Court of Justice may participate tacitly in this process of informal norm development. It might be more accurate to attribute the judgment in the German wine case to a promise that was extended to Germany than to think of it in terms of the administrative regularity cited by the Court. At the time that the Federal Republic agreed to a high duty on wines, the *quid pro quo* was that requests for special quotas would be received favorably. Leon N. Lindberg, *The Political Dynamics of European Economic Integration* (Stanford, California: Stanford University Press, 1963), pp. 216–217.

61. 7, 13, 20, 25, 27, 28, 31/61 Molkerei-Centrale Westfalen/Lippe GmbH *et al.* v. Hauptzollamt Paderborn *et al.*, 7 *C.M.L.R.* 187 — 3 and 4 April 68.

62. *Ibid.*, (20/67 Firma Kunstmühle Tivoli v. Hauptzollamt Würzburg), p. 236. (italics added).

63. Article 177 (b), E.E.C. Treaty.

64. 5/67 W. Beus GmbH & Co. v. Hauptzollamt München-Landerberstrasse, 7 *C.M.L.R.* 131, 150 — 13 March 68.

65. See 19/68 De Cicco v. Landesversicherungsanstalt Schwaben, 8 *C.M.L.R.* 67 — 19 December 68. In this case a German judge asked the Court for an authoritative interpretation of a provision of Com-

munity social policy, since he disagreed with a decision on the matter by another German judge.

66. European Commission, *Third General Report on the Activities of the Communities 1969*, pp. 47–48. The reference is to 2 & 3/69 Sociaal Fonds voor Diamente arbeiders v. SA Ch. Brachfeld & Sons *et al.*, *ibid.*, p. 474.

67. 20/64 Albatros s.a.r.l. v. Société des Pétroles et des Combustibles Liquides (SOPÉCO), 4 *C.M.L.R.* 159 — 4 February 65.

68. Court of Justice, "Statistiques Mensuelles" (to July 1, 1970).

69. See, among others, 11/67 Office National des Pensions pour Ouvriers v. Couture, 7 *C.M.L.R.* 14 — 12 December 67.

70. 5/69 Franz Volk v. Ets. Vervaecke S.P.R.L., 8 *C.M.L.R.* 273, 282 — 9 July 69.

71. The tradition is strongest in the United States, but this was also one of the areas of Coal and Steel Community litigation where the Court of Justice displayed a real taste for policymaking. See Scheingold, *The Rule of Law*, Chapter 13.

72. On the nature of federal ordering, see *supra*, pp. 26–27.

73. There are groups excluded from the decisionmaking process, and their exclusion is, in effect, reinforced by consistent validation. For these "outsiders" the process is, then, coercive rather than consensual. But it is the technocratic rather than the federal features of the Community system that are thus underscored. See Stuart A. Scheingold, "Domestic and International Consequences of Regional Integration," *International Organization*, Vol. 24, No. 4 (Autumn 1970), pp. 993–994.

74. Lindberg and Scheingold, *Europe's Would-Be Polity*, p. 119.

75. *Ibid.*

76. *Ibid.*

77. *Aperçu des travaux de la Cour de justice des Communautés européennes* (Luxembourg: Publications Department of the European Communities, 1970).

78. One recalls *Time's* comment about one key meeting of the Council on agricultural policy. "The sessions were heated. Three officials collapsed with heart attacks, and stubble-bearded, trigger-tempered delegates fought long into the night, stoked with double whiskies brought to the conference table . . . 'This isn't integration!' shouted a Netherlands minister, 'This is disintegration!'" Quoted in Leon N. Lindberg, *The Political Dynamics of European Economic Integration*, p. 289.

79. The discrepancy between these figures and those in Table 1 is due to the fact that the earlier table includes suits filed while this involves decisions rendered.

80. For a discussion of the nature and limits of that discretion, see Peter Hay, "Supremacy of Community Law in National Courts," *American Journal of Comparative Law*, Vol. 16 (1968), pp. 526–532.

81. *Ibid.*, p. 535.

82. Article 177 (2).

83. It should be noted that there is no official procedure for collecting data on national litigation which involves Community law. The Court of Justice freely admits this and appeals for information on such decisions from any and all sources. See *Aperçu des travaux de la Cour de justice des Communautés européennes*, p. 11, footnote 1.

84. For a thorough but rather unsympathetic briefing on these points, see Hay, "Supremacy of Community Law," pp. 526–532.

85. Re Société des Pétroles Shell-Berre and others, French Conseil d'Etat, 3 *C.M.L.R.* 462, 481–483 — 19 June 64.

86. Hay, "Supremacy of Community Law," p. 551. The discussion which follows is drawn primarily from this article.

87. Richard M. Buxbaum, "Article 177 of the Rome Treaty as a Federalizing Device," *Stanford Law Review*, Vol. 21, No. 4 (May 1969), pp. 1043–1045.

88. Hay, "Supremacy of Community Law," p. 549. The initial Article 177 proceeding to reach the Court of Justice from the Conseil d'Etat was 34/70 Syndicat national du commerce extérieur des céréales et autres v. l'office national interprofessionnel des céréales et M. le Ministre de l'agriculture, *Journal officiel des Communautés européennes*, 15.8. 70, No. C105/13.

89. Caisse Régionale de Sécurité Sociale du Nord-Est v. Goffart, French Cour de Cassation, 8 *C.M.L.R.* 24–25 — 21 March 68.

90. Hay, "Supremacy of Community Law," pp. 544–547.

91. Recall the German judge who sent forward a question to the Court of Justice in order to clear up inconsistencies in interpretation among German courts.

92. Buxbaum, "Article 177 of the Rome Treaty," p. 1045.

93. *Ibid.*, p. 1054.

94. A study of this sort should not, it seems to me, ignore the important question raised by the German fiscal court — the status of national constitutional guarantees under Community law. Artcle 177 procedures may open up new avenues of relief, but if the supremacy doctrine is used to foreclose fundamental protections the net loss in democratic values is obvious. The Community system is dangerously vulnerable on these grounds and research on legal interpenetration should look beyond its integrative effects to whatever consequences it may have in extending technocratic procedures at the expense of democratic values. See Scheingold, "Domestic and International Consequences," pp. 991–995.

95. European Commission, *Third General Report on the Activities of the Communities 1969* (Brussels-Luxembourg: Publications Department of the European Communities, 1970), p. 455. Peter Hay also discusses an appeal procedure, in "Supremacy of Community Law," p. 551.

96. As the project finally materialized, I interviewed a total of fifty-nine attorneys in five of the six member-countries (excluding Luxembourg). I can not claim that this group is in any precise sense a representative sampling, since my technique amounted to contacting every attorney who had been involved in litigation before the Court

of Justice (through the fall of 1964) and making further contacts largely through them. Given these rather *ad hoc* procedures, my results can be considered no more than a pilot project. The attorneys with whom I spoke were, however, extremely cooperative — often allowing me three hours or more of their time and thus giving me considerable "feeling" for the way in which they perceived and performed their role in the Community system.

97. One could alternatively consider the attorneys themselves as a key elite, although this premise is probably less tenable in Europe than it might be in America. But this approach would presumably have called for a consideration of all attorneys and required a different kind of interview schedule. Some of my data are, nevertheless, suggestive in these terms and seem to indicate that attorneys, as a profession, may develop a distinctive, if not altogether uniform, set of attitudes towards European integration.

98. Talcott Parsons, "The Law and Social Control," in William N. Evan, ed., *Law and Sociology* (Glencoe, Ill.: Free Press, 1962), p. 63.

99. Geoffrey Sawer, *Law in Society* (Oxford: Oxford University Press, 1965), p. 7.

100. As of January 1, 1970, 9,266 notifications were pending before the Commission; 13,810 agreements had been cleared during 1969 alone. Of the enforcement actions pending on January 1, 1970, 70 were undertaken as a result of Commission investigation, while 71 resulted from complaints from business firms. I was assured in an interview that the rather small enforcement staff of the antitrust division must count upon complaints from firms to uncover violations. European Commission, *Third General Report on the Activities of the Communities 1969*, p. 61.

101. It should be pointed out that when these interviews were conducted, the full import of Article 177 as it has been presented in this paper was not really clear. One might hazard the guess that satisfaction with this procedure, particularly in combination with national litigation, would be considerably higher today.

102. It is important not to exaggerate the position of the European attorney. He is not as likely as his American counterpart would probably be to negotiate or bargain for his client with the bureaucracy. The strongly negative reaction of attorneys to the bureaucracy may, therefore, represent an uninformed reaction rather than an experienced judgment. Indeed, some of the data presented earlier suggest that in technical terms the bureaucracy may be developing reliable guides.

103. The extent to which the attorney's longrange commitment tends to undermine his inclination for vigorous advocacy, at least in given cases, has been well documented by students of the American criminal justice system.

104. Eric Stein makes a similar point in a different context. "In the long run, perhaps the most pervasive result of the process of assimilation of laws in this field will be the progressive socialization of elite actors who, by the very nature of their profession, have traditionally operated

[58]

in a territorially intensive network within a nation-State. The elite includes law trained national and transnational officials, law professors, attorneys, and business counsel plus parliamentarians and spokesmen for economic and professional interest groups." Eric Stein, *Harmonization of European Company Law: National Reform and Transnational Coordination* (Indianapolis, Ind.: Bobbs-Merrill, 1971), p. 511.

105. It was shocking to discover from time to time how little some lawyers knew about Community law. What was apparent to me as a layman is no doubt even clearer to officials in Brussels and Luxembourg.

106. *Aperçu des travaux de la Cour de justice*, p. 18.

107. *Ibid.*, p. 19.

RECENT BOOKS WRITTEN UNDER THE CENTER'S AUSPICES

Development Policy: Theory and Practice, ed. G. F. Papanek, 1968. Harvard University Press. ISBN 0–674–20250–3.

Political Order in Changing Societies, by Samuel P. Huntington, 1968. Yale University Press. ISBN 0–300–00584–4.

Aid, Influence, and Foreign Policy, by Joan M. Nelson, 1968. Macmillan.

International Regionalism, by Joseph S. Nye, Jr., 1968. Little, Brown & Co. 617334.

Turmoil and Transition: Higher Education and Student Politics in India, ed. Philip G. Altbach, 1968. Lalvani Publishing House, Bombay 1.

The TFX Decision: McNamara and the Military, by Robert J. Art, 1968. Little, Brown & Co. 052418.

Korea: The Politics of the Vortex, by Gregory Henderson, 1968. Harvard University Press. ISBN 0–674–50550–6.

The Precarious Republic, by Michael C. Hudson, 1968. Random House. ISBN 0–674–30287.

Political Development in Latin America, by Martin Needler, 1968. Random House. ISBN 0–674–30446.

Revolution and Counterrevolution: Change and Persistence in Social Structures, by Seymour Martin Lipset, 1968. Basic Books. ISBN 0–465–06953–3.

Agrarian Socialism, by S. M. Lipset, revised edition, 1968. Doubleday-Anchor Books.

The Brazilian Capital Goods Industry, 1929–1964, by Nathaniel H. Leff, 1968. Harvard University Press. ISBN 0–674–08090–4.

Economic Policy-Making and Development in Brazil, 1947–1964, by Nathaniel H. Leff, 1968. Wiley.

German Foreign Policy in Transition, by Karl Kaiser, 1968. Oxford University Press. ISBN 0–19–285025–3.

Taxation and Development: Lessons from Colombian Experience, by Richard M. Bird, 1969. Harvard University Press. ISBN 0–674–86840–4.

The Process of Modernization: An Annotated Bibliography on the Socio-cultural Aspects of Development, by John Brode, 1969. Harvard University Press. ISBN 0–674–71070–3.

Protest and Power in Black Africa, eds. Robert I. Rotberg and Ali A. Mazrui, 1970. Oxford University Press.

Agricultural Development in India's Districts: The Intensive Agricultural Districts Programme, by Dorris D. Brown, 1970. Harvard University Press. SBN 674–01230–5.

Korean Development: The Interplay of Politics and Economics, by David

[60]

C. Cole and Princeton N. Lyman, 1970. Harvard University Press. SBN 674–50563–8.

Europe's Would-Be Polity, by Leon Lindberg and Stuart A. Scheingold, 1970. Prentice-Hall.

Peace in Europe, by Karl E. Birnbaum, 1970. Oxford University Press. ISBN 0–19–2850432.

Lord and Peasant in Peru, by F. LaMond Tullis, 1970. Harvard University Press. ISBN 0–674–53914–1.

Authoritarian Politics in Modern Society: The Dynamics of Established One-Party Systems, eds. Samuel P. Huntington and Clement H. Moore, 1970. Basic Books. ISBN 465–00569–1.

The Logic of Images in International Relations, by Robert Jervis, 1970. Princeton University Press. 07532–8.

Nuclear Diplomacy, by George H. Quester, 1970. The Dunellen Co., Inc.

Political Mobilization of the Venezuelan Peasant, by John D. Powell, 1971. Harvard University Press. ISBN 0–674–68626–8.

International Norms and War between States: Three Studies in International Politics, by Kjell Goldman, 1971. Läromedelsförlagen (Sweden) and the Swedish Institute of International Affairs.

The Kennedy Round in American Trade Policy, by John W. Evans, 1971. Harvard University Press. SBN 674–50275–2.

Studies in Development Planning, ed. Hollis B. Chenery, 1971. Harvard University Press.

Peace in Parts? Regional Organizations, Integration, and Conflict, by Joseph S. Nye, 1971. Little, Brown & Co.

The Myth of the Guerrilla, by J. Bowyer Bell, forthcoming from Blond (London) and Knopf (New York).

Sovereignty at Bay: The Multinational Spread of U.S. Enterprise, by Raymond Vernon, forthcoming from Basic Books.

Development Policy II: The Pakistan Experience, eds. Walter P. Falcon and Gustav F. Papanek, forthcoming from Harvard University Press.

Latin American University Students. A Six Nation Comparative Study, by Arthur Liebman *et al.*, forthcoming from Harvard University Press.

Peasants against Politics: Rural Organization in Brittany, 1911–1967, by Suzanne Berger, forthcoming from Harvard University Press.

The Politics of Land Reform in Chile, 1950–1970, by Robert R. Kaufman, forthcoming from Harvard University Press.

OCCASIONAL PAPERS IN INTERNATIONAL AFFAIRS

1. *A Plan for Planning: The Need for a Better Method of Assisting Under-developed Countries on Their Economic Policies,* by Gustav F. Papanek, 1961. 12 pp. $.25.
2. *The Flow of Resources from Rich to Poor,* by Alan D. Neale, 1961. Out of print.
3. *Limited War: An Essay on the Development of the Theory and an Annotated Bibliography,* by Morton H. Halperin, 1962. Out of print.
4. *Reflections on the Failure of the First West Indian Federation,* by Hugh W. Springer, 1962. Out of print.
5. *On the Interaction of Opposing Forces under Possible Arms Agreements,* by Glenn A. Kent, 1963. 36 pp. $1. ISBN 0–87674–001–8.
6. *Europe's Northern Cap and the Soviet Union,* by Nils Örvik, 1963. 64 pp. $1. ISBN 0–87674–002–6.
7. *Civil Administration in the Punjab: An Analysis of a State Government in India,* by E. N. Mangat Rai, 1963. 82 pp. $1. ISBN 0–87674–003–2.
8. *On the Appropriate Size of a Development Program,* by Edward S. Mason, 1964. 24 pp. 75 cents. ISBN 0–87674–004–2.
9. *Self-Determination Revisited in the Era of Decolonization,* by Rupert Emerson, 1964. 64 pp. $1.25. ISBN 0–87674–005–0.
10. *The Planning and Execution of Economic Development in Southeast Asia,* by Clair Wilcox, 1965. 27 pp. $1. ISBN 0–87674–006–9.
11. *Pan-Africanism in Action,* by Albert Tevoedjre, 1965. 88 pp. $2. ISBN 0–87674–007–7.
12. *Is China Turning In?* by Morton H. Halperin, 1965. 34 pp. $1. ISBN 0–87674–008–5.
13. *Economic Development in India and Pakistan,* by Edward S. Mason, 1966. Out of print.
14. *The Role of the Military in Recent Turkish Politics,* by Ergun Özbudun, 1966. 54 pp. $1.25. ISBN 0–87674–009–3.
15. *Economic Development and Individual Change: A Social-Psychological Study of the Comilla Experiment in Pakistan,* by Howard Schuman, 1967. Out of print.
16. *A Select Bibliography on Students, Politics, and Higher Education,* by Philip G. Altbach, 1967. 54 pp. $2.50. ISBN 0–87674–011–5.
17. *Europe's Political Puzzle: A Study of the Fouchet Negotiations and the 1963 Veto,* by Alessandro Silj, 1967. 178 pp. $2.50. ISBN 0–87674–012–3.
18. *The Cap and the Straits: Problems of Nordic Security,* by Jan Klenberg, 1968. 19 pp. $1. ISBN 0–87674–013–1.

[62]

19. *Cyprus: The Law and Politics of Civil Strife*, by Linda B. Miller, 1968. 97 pp. $2.50. ISBN 0–87674–014–X.
20. *East and West Pakistan: A Problem in the Political Economy of Regional Planning*, by Md. Anisur Rahman, 1968. 38 pp. $2. ISBN 0–87674–015–8.
21. *Internal War and International Systems: Perspectives on Method*, by George A. Kelly and Linda B. Miller, 1969. 40 pp. $2. ISBN 0–87674–016–6.
22. *Migrants, Urban Poverty, and Instability in Developing Nations*, by Joan M. Nelson, 1969. 83 pp. $2.25. ISBN 0–87674–017–4.
23. *Growth and Development in Pakistan, 1955–1969*, by Joseph J. Stern and Walter P. Falcon, 1970. 94 pp. $2.75. ISBN 0–87674–018–2.
24. *Higher Education in Developing Countries: A Select Bibliography*, by Philip G. Altbach, 1970. 118 pp. $3.75. ISBN 0–87674–019–0.
25. *Anatomy of Political Institutionalization: The Case of Israel and Some Comparative Analyses*, by Amos Perlmutter, 1970. 60 pp. $2.25. ISBN 0–87674–020–4.
26. *The German Democratic Republic from the Sixties to the Seventies*, by Peter C. Ludz, 1970. 100 pp. $3.00. ISBN 0–87674–021–2.
27. *The Law in Political Integration: The Evolution and Integrative Implications of Regional Legal Processes in the European Community*, by Stuart A. Scheingold, 1971. 59 pp. $2.25. ISBN 0–87674–022–0.
28. *Conflict Regulation in Divided Societies*, by Eric A. Nordlinger, forthcoming.

J7